Other Books by Jerry Izenberg

Nonfiction:

Baseball, Nazis and Nedick's Hot Dogs: Growing Up Jewish in the 1930s in Newark

Once There Were Giants: The Golden Age of Heavyweight Boxing

Rozelle: A Biography

Through My Eyes: A Sportswriter's 58-Year Journey

No Medals for Trying

The Jerry Izenberg Collection

Championship: The NFL Title Story

How Many Miles to Camelot: The All-American Sports Myth

New York Giants: Seventy-Five Years

The Greatest Game Ever Played

At Large With Jerry Izenberg

The Rivals

Great Latin Sports Figures

Fiction:

After the Fire: Love and Hate in the Ashes of 1967

LARRY DOBY

IN BLACK AND WHITE

LARRY DOBY
IN BLACK AND WHITE

THE STORY OF A BASEBALL PIONEER

JERRY IZENBERG

Sports Publishing books may be purchased in bulk at special discounts for sales promotion, corporate gifts, fund-raising, or educational purposes. Special editions can also be created to specifications. For details, contact the Special Sales Department, Sports Publishing, 307 West 36th Street, 11th Floor, New York, NY 10018 or sportspubbooks@skyhorsepublishing.com.

Sports Publishing® is a registered trademark of Skyhorse Publishing, Inc.®, a Delaware corporation.

Visit our website at www.sportspubbooks.com.

10 9 8 7 6 5 4 3 2

Library of Congress Cataloging-in-Publication Data is available on file.

Cover design by David Ter-Avaneysan
Cover photo credit: Getty Images

Print ISBN: 978-1-68358-480-3
Ebook ISBN: 978-1-68358-481-0

Printed in the United States of America

To the family of my friend Larry Doby.

And the memory of those born too soon to be his major-league teammates.

TABLE OF CONTENTS

PROLOGUE

In 1967, I was the lead sports columnist with the *Newark Star-Ledger*, and our circulation was based around greater New York—the only area in the country that once had three major-league baseball teams. Cleveland is five hundred road miles from New York City. We had the Yankees, the Dodgers, and the Giants. Cleveland had the Indians—a team that had won only one World Series in the previous twenty-eight years.

That hardly engendered the ingredients for the kind of rivalry that would necessitate my going to Cleveland to cover Larry Doby. I would see him occasionally when the Indians came to Yankee Stadium, though our relationship did not go much further than "Hi, Larry." "Hi, Jerry."

But when I answered my front door on a snowy night in 1976, I was stunned to see him standing there. I had no idea why.

"Hey," I said. "What's up?"

"What do you drink?" he asked.

"Honestly, if it's wet, I'll drink it."

"I'll see you at seven tonight."

And then he disappeared—a lone figure in the falling snow. Until then I really hadn't thought about the fact that we both lived in the same town of Montclair, New Jersey. That afternoon, I thought, *Well, I am his hometown columnist in the off-season. Maybe I had written something he didn't like.* I never considered the fact that I had written more about social issues than any columnist at any paper in his circulation area. Even though he had won in court, I still had to defend Muhammad Ali's decision not to serve during the Vietnam War. So what did Doby want?

That night triggered a friendship that lasted more than three decades.

Years later I decided to write this book, and for three reasons. First, I still miss him. Second, our mutual friend, the late Monte Irvin, his infield mate on the Newark Eagles and in the National Baseball Hall of Fame, convinced me I needed to do it. And third, in 2020, Doby's son, Larry Jr., gave me a clue for what might have prompted his dad's late-night winter visit. I still have no definite answer, but Larry Jr. told me that the reason might have been this: "My dad had a hard life. I know that he didn't trust many people, but he trusted you. If you are going to write a book, I'll give you any help I can. Just ask."

Doby Sr. arrived right on time the night we first got to know each other. As promised, he brought a bottle of scotch. We sat down at the kitchen table. We didn't get up until the bottle was mortally wounded and the sun was high in the sky.

That long day's night was for me a long-overdue awakening—and for him, I believe, a kind of exorcism. I think he read a lot of my columns before he decided to come see me because, without my asking, he told me things he had kept deep inside him for years. The way it felt alone at night in Black boardinghouses in the sweltering heat of summer on the road, with no air conditioning except for a block of ice on a table with a small fan blowing against it in a losing battle . . . the voice of a racist fan in St. Louis as he stood in the first row insulting Doby's wife. Doby even tried to climb into the grandstand to fight him, though pitching coach Bill McKechnie stopped him (McKechnie is quoted as saying to Doby, "Don't go up there, kid. That will ruin you, not him.") . . . the beer cans that crowds threw at him during his first spring-training swing through the South . . . the beanballs disguised as inside pitches that he ducked.

While Jackie Robinson did a much-publicized apprentice season in Canada with the Dodgers' farm team, the Montreal Royals, Doby labored in relative obscurity with the segregated Newark Eagles of the all-Black Negro National League. White baseball fans knew who Jackie was before he got there. Of more importance was the Dodgers' advance public promise that Jackie would be the chosen one, the first. And by spring training 1947, he was.

The same white fans had never heard of Larry Doby.

Two years after the two pioneers made their debuts, New York Giants skipper Leo Durocher announced the integration of his club in a way that shut off all possible protests. He did something Lou Boudreau, the Cleveland Indians manager, never even thought about.

Durocher stood in the middle of a pregame locker room and shouted, "Hey, pay attention! These two Black guys are on our team now. Monte Irvin could be one of the greatest hitters this franchise ever had, and Hank Thompson can play the infield and the outfield. I expect to win a pennant, and soon, with these guys. If you don't like that, then you can just go fuck yourselves."

Nobody dared say a word.

When Doby left the Newark Eagles in July 1947, he was leading the Negro National League with a .354 batting average and eight home runs. But that was light years away from the American League. As far as the men he was about to meet were concerned, he might as well have been playing in Iceland. Virtually nobody in that Cleveland locker room had ever heard anything about him.

But it was no secret that he wasn't a white man.

Upon Doby's signing, Boudreau gave a very PC response to the United Press. "Doby will be given every chance to prove that he has the ability to make good with us. The reports we have received on this ability are outstanding. I hope he can succeed as he has with other teams."

Unfortunately for Larry, that sentiment was not shared with those in the locker room, and his inactions spoke louder than his words.

Doby, the first Black man to play in an American League game, always felt Boudreau didn't want him—and certainly the manager gave him no reason to change that impression during that first day. He said nothing more, instead giving credence to what he left unsaid.

There were twenty-five players and three coaches on the team. Only five of them faced Doby and offered legitimate handshakes: catcher Jim Hegan; second baseman and future Hall of Famer Joe Gordon, who would become one of Doby's lifelong friends; pitchers Bob Lemon and Steve Gromek; and pitching coach Bill McKechnie.

Doby later told me that after those five men, he got "mostly dead-fishes" handshakes. And two of them, first basemen Eddie Robinson and Les Fleming, turned their backs to him completely.

Yet after that disastrous introduction, the manager was shrewd and self-serving enough to tell the Cleveland media, "This is a routine baseball signing. Creed, race, or color have no [negative] role in baseball."

Obviously, he knew that was light years from the truth. Boudreau apparently did not want him, Doby felt sure of that. But was it racism? Fear that his team would rebel and he would lose control? Or simply the idea that Larry was signed as an infielder and with Boudreau at short and Joe Gordon as an All-Star second baseman, where was he going to play Doby?

I never knew any of this while Doby was an active player. He wasn't Jackie Robinson. He was Larry Doby, and sportswriters of the era seemed to think he was just a case of redundancy. They were wrong. Their preconceived notion was enough to send this American hero into the black hole of history, mostly forgotten.

If Doby was the victim of a stacked deck, the man who attempted to bring justice to the game was Joe Gordon.

"Right after those strained introductions," Doby recalled, "I'm walking through the tunnel and through the dugout and onto the field. And they are already out there warming up—all of them. I'm standing alone and nobody—I mean nobody—will throw me the ball. And I'm thinking, *The hell with them. I don't need this*. And just then somebody elbows me in the ribs and I turn with my fists up and, yeah, I'm ready to fight.

"It's Joe Gordon. And he's laughing, and he says, 'Rookie, are you ready to warm up or do you want to just stand there in your brand-new uniform and profile?' And, you know, from that moment for as long we both were Indians, we warmed up that way—together, just the two of us—before every game we played."

On July 5, in his first career game in the major leagues, Boudreau sent Doby up in the seventh inning as a pinch-hitter against the White Sox. He had never faced major-league pitching before. He saw five pitches. He got around early on the second one and drove a vicious shot down the right-field line, but it faded and curved foul. He struck out. Frustrated, he dropped his bat and walked slowly into the dugout and sat at the end of the bench, as far away from the manager as he could get. He sat alone with his head down. He sat there a lot that year, isolated except for the many times Gordon deliberately got up and walked over to sit next to him.

Boudreau barely used him that first year. He appeared in just 29 games, mostly as a pinch-hitter or a pinch-runner, and had just five hits in thirty-two at-bats. In fact, of those 29 games, he only played one from beginning to end, and had only one at-bat or less in 24 of those 29 games.

The hottest hitter in the Negro National League on the day he left to join the Indians, he felt a blend of anger and embarrassment. He had never experienced a season this bad in his life.

At the end of the 1947 season, Jackie Robinson was a genuine Black baseball hero, taking home Rookie of the Year honors. Larry Doby was simply a footnote, written off by a manager who didn't want him. I never read anything about his disastrous year. I never saw much about it in the New York or New Jersey newspapers, never read anything about it from the wire services—except that several Cleveland writers thought he should be released or sent to the minor leagues.

I never knew the story until years later, when I sat with Larry at my kitchen table on a dark, snowy night.

Later, the more research I did, the more I wondered how the story of his lonely battle was allowed to slip through the cracks for years until it almost seemed headed toward oblivion.

I learned he had been asked about that a lot, and he always answered, "They had written a lot about Mr. Robinson and just didn't want to write the same old story all over again." It reminded me of a question I once asked and how forcefully he had answered. Anger was reflected in his voice when he said, "No. I never thought of quitting. Not once."

This is his story—the way men who later became my colleagues never chose to write it.

LARRY DOBY

IN BLACK AND WHITE

CHAPTER 1

CLEVELAND AIN'T BROOKLYN

On July 4, 1947, Larry Doby said goodbye to the Negro National League with a single powerful swing of his bat that sent the ball soaring toward and into the right field stands at Newark's Ruppert Stadium. That won the first game of a doubleheader against the Philadelphia Stars.

When the teams returned for the second game, Doby was already on a train headed for Chicago, accompanied by Lou Jones, a member of the Cleveland Indians' public-relations staff.

Doby never told me what he was thinking when he began his final home-run trot in a Newark Eagles uniform, but everyone in the stands and his teammates waiting to greet him at home plate knew the moment was special.

He wasn't running toward home. He was running toward history. He was running toward a place no Black man before him had ever gone.

Within twenty-four hours, he would integrate the American League. And from the very beginning, most of the players, most of the fans, and virtually all the baseball writers couldn't begin to grasp the actual impact of his journey. Cleveland of 1947 wasn't Brooklyn of 1947, where Jackie Robinson broke the National League color line. Despite later revisionist history, Lou Boudreau, the manager of the Cleveland Indians, was hardly a disciple of what critics snidely referred to as "Bill Veeck's experiment." The American League of 1947 had no interest in any kind of diversity.

In truth, until Jackie Robinson was the first to shatter the color line—on Opening Day in 1947—neither did the National League. Not since May 1, 1884, when Moses Fleetwood Walker played for the Toledo Blue Stockings, had a Black man played as much as a single inning in "organized baseball." Only four years before Robinson broke the color line, baseball ownership and its commissioner, Judge Kenesaw Mountain Landis, met behind closed doors to secretly reaffirm their unwritten agreement to maintain segregation.

Landis had been a federal judge in 1919 when eight members of the Chicago White Sox ("Black Sox"), funded by the notorious gambler Arnold Rothstein, were suspected of deliberately losing the World Series. Baseball owners panicked. They knew they had lost public trust. Gate receipts nosedived the following year.

Even the arrogant men who comprised major-league ownership had understood their image as America's "national pastime" was in danger. Out of a blend of panic and fear, they hired Landis as their first commissioner, installing absolute power in the new position. He banned the eight players from the game forever. He was baseball's sole, unquestioned ruler for twenty-four years, and a vital force in keeping baseball white.

On December 3, 1943, Landis chaired a closed-door meeting in Conference Room O of New York's Hotel Roosevelt to respond to growing pressure to integrate. The Brotherhood of United Pulman Porters, the Communist Party newspaper (the *Daily Worker*), and groups of activists displayed their support for the integration of Major League Baseball with a parade through the heart of Manhattan on Fifth Avenue for thirty-six blocks.

African American actor Paul Robeson, then starring on Broadway in *Othello*, had gone to Landis's secret meeting as an invited guest to reason with the owners.

Speaking on the record to Robeson and a distinguished Black delegation, Landis bitingly said, "Maybe I don't know what's going on here. I don't know about and I won't testify to that [unwritten agreement to maintain segregation] after all I have learned in 23 years [as commissioner]. There is no way I would testify to such an agreement. God knows these men [*pointing to the owners*] are not cowardly enough not to put it on paper, and I am not crook enough to enforce it.

"Now, do you understand that?" There was clear menace in his attitude.

"No way," he added, "would anyone enforce it."

But they did—and so did he.

His words were a ploy to avoid responsibility for what clearly was an effective silent agreement of six decades. They were spoken at a time when American Blacks were dying along with whites on World War II battlefields in Europe and Asia—and a time when Black activists were uniting in a rebuttal of Landis's words, using the slogan "If they can stop bullets, they can stop baseballs."

But Landis remained firmly committed to defending the Caucasian purity of what he considered "his game," and the lie that he blatantly told Robeson never bothered him. He maintained his closed-door policy until the day he died, in 1944.

Four years later, new commissioner and former US Senator Happy Chandler opened that same door to both Robinson and Doby.

What even the media never understood was that Larry Doby's debut, six weeks after Robinson's, was not simply a rewriting of the second coming of Jackie Robinson.

What it was . . . was the first coming of Larry Doby.

He was the right guy at the right time in the wrong place. Nobody in the American League, including the team for which he would play, sent a welcome wagon to greet him. George Weiss, the general manager of America's team (the perennial champion New York Yankees), when asked if the Yankees were interested in signing a Black player, told the media, "Our fans are different. Do you think a Wall Street stockbroker would buy season box-seat tickets to see a colored boy play for us?"

Here was the GM of the world's most famous baseball team expressing absolutely no interest in either bringing his team into the immediate social flow of the twentieth century nor in utilizing an untapped source of talent to help maintain the team's consistent excellence. It took eight more years before Elston Howard became the first Black man to wear a Yankees uniform, and another four for the Boston Red Sox to sign their first African American, an infielder named Pumpsie Green, and finally complete the reluctant integration of the American League.

But in the beginning for both leagues, there were only two. Two lonely ballplayers against an establishment of bigotry, fear of the unknown, and blatant white racism. There was Doby, unwanted by most of his teammates and his own manager, and Robinson, whom the Dodgers had to send to their Montreal farm team to ease some of the massive groundswell of homegrown racism generated when he signed.

What both had to fight was typified by an episode during Robinson's 1946 spring training with Montreal. Robinson made a spectacular play, and Dodgers owner Branch Rickey said to Montreal manager Clay Hopper that no human could have made that play. Hopper, born and raised in racially segregated Mississippi, replied, "Mr. Rickey, do you really think a nigra is a human being?"

Larry and Jackie—two pioneers with the same problem. In addition to their natural talent, they shared three qualities that gave them their tickets to ride the first underground railroad in baseball history. Both had competed most of their lives with and against white players, both had been to college (Doby at Long Island University and Virginia Union, Robinson at UCLA), and both had served in World War II (Army and Navy, respectively). Those were serious credentials with which to break the color line.

But beyond that, they were clearly different. To understand the difference, you first must understand that Doby was not Robinson—not in temperament, nor in the environment that produced him. Of even more importance, during his rookie season Doby was never backed by the strong support system Robinson received.

When Ben Chapman, the Phillies' racist manager and one of baseball's most vicious bench jockeys, stood on the dugout steps screaming "Nigger! Nigger!" at Robinson, Dodgers second baseman Eddie Stanky raced across the field and tried to punch him out. When Cincinnati Reds fans jeered and booed him before a game, Dodgers shortstop and captain Pee Wee Reese walked over to a surprised Robinson, draped an arm around his shoulders, and told him, "Laugh at me like we're sharing a joke. The heck with those people."

But when an infielder on the Philadelphia Athletics spit tobacco juice into Doby's face while sliding into second base, nobody rushed off the Indians bench to defend him.

Jackie played football and baseball at UCLA. In 1937 and 1938, he played in front of 90,000 people in the Rose Bowl. His exploits were covered by the Los Angeles newspapers. Additionally, he had secret tryouts with the Chicago Cubs and Boston Red Sox in response to the growing pressure generated against baseball's secret policy of "no Negroes." The Boston tryout was the result of a city councilman's threat to use the city's "blue laws" to end the Red Sox's ability to play lucrative Sunday doubleheaders. The tryouts in both cities were actually little more than self-protective charades by both teams.

Later, newspaper readers across the country would know all about Robinson's well-reported year with the Montreal Royals. When he led them to the International League title, fans carried him off the field in salute. It may have been one of the first times in which a mob of white people chased an American Black man just to hug him.

He was a headliner in the major-league spotlight in a city that, for the most part, welcomed him. But in Cleveland, Doby was stepping into a far different situation.

Unlike in Brooklyn, Cleveland schools were still segregated. Restaurants either overcharged or refused to serve Black patrons. Movie theaters confined them to the balcony. Amusement parks like Euclid Beach Park were off limits to them by a mutually understood, unwritten agreement. Only after intense pressure was City Hospital desegregated.

To compound the city's uneasy race relations, its changing demographics were considered hostile in the many enclaves originally settled by European immigrants. A flood of Black migrants, lured to Cleveland from the Deep South by the prospect of World War II factory jobs, were shuttled off to a single overcrowded ghetto, the Central-Woodland area. The lack of available housing for them was real and hostility fueled.

Better housing for Blacks with better paying jobs became available only through the efforts of unscrupulous blockbusting real estate agents who triggered white flight with rumors and worse.

"If you looked at Cleveland back then," boxing promoter Don King (who was born in Cleveland) told me, "you really were looking at two divided and totally different cities in one—socially and economically. There were lines you just didn't cross back then, and we knew it."

Therefore, unlike Robinson's debut, Doby's arrival was not greeted with ruffles and flourishes. His entire professional career had been spent in the segregated and lightly reported confines of the Negro National League, with the Newark Eagles. Most of the time, both the *Newark Star-Ledger* and the *Newark Evening News* didn't even bother to print' box scores of their games.

Thinking about the advantages that Brooklyn, and New York City in general, offered a Black player trying to shatter the color line, Cleveland comes off as a distant long shot.

Bill Veeck, the Indians' owner, was a rebel who had often waged a guerrilla war against baseball ownership's old guard. As a case in point, there was his attempt to buy the failing Philadelphia Phillies.

Since 1918, the Phillies had just one winning season. They were also deeply in debt to the league. Landis, the baseball commissioner, was out of patience. He ordered the owner, Gerry Nugent, to sell the franchise immediately.

What Landis had learned was that Veeck planned to sign a number of stars from the Negro Leagues in open defiance of an ironclad color line that Landis continually claimed did not exist.

In his autobiography, *Veeck—As in Wreck*, his goal in making an offer for the Phillies was to be as transparent with the commissioner as possible in terms of his intentions.

"I made one bad mistake," Veeck said in his book. "Out of my long respect for Judge Landis I felt he was entitled to prior notification of what I intended to do. I was aware of the risk I was taking although, to be honest, I could not see how he could stop me. The color line was a 'gentleman's agreement' only. The only way the Commissioner could bar me from using Negroes would be to rule, officially and publicly, that they were 'detrimental to baseball.' With Negroes fighting in the war, such a ruling was unthinkable.

"Judge Landis wasn't exactly shocked but he wasn't exactly overjoyed either. His first reaction, in fact, was that I was kidding him."

"My dad," his son Mike Veeck told me, "made the highest bid. That's a fact. But it was sold to Bill Cox, who later was banned for gambling on baseball. Dad never said who undercut his bid for the Phillies, but it's no mystery. The owners and the commissioner railroaded him."

But later, with Landis gone, Veeck and his respected partner, future Hall of Famer Hank Greenberg, bought the Cleveland Indians and signed Doby as the second Black player in Major League Baseball.

"Robinson had proven he was a genuine major leaguer," Veeck would say. "I wanted to get the best available Negro boys while the grabbing was good. Why wait? In 10 years, they will be in service with many big-league teams because there are many colored players with sufficient capabilities to play in the major leagues."

"I think my grandfather had a lot to do with Dad's attitude," Mike Veeck told me. "He was the president of the Chicago Cubs and he often brought visitors like John McGraw [the Giants' feisty manager] home to dinner. It was my grandfather who instilled a love of the game in my dad and an understanding of the business as well.

"One day he took my dad into the counting room behind the box office at Wrigley Field. He asked what color the money was, and Dad said it was green. Then he asked what color were the people who put that money into the room. And Dad said, 'I guess all colors.'

"My father told me that story, and then he looked at me and said, 'Remember that.'"

Veeck signed Doby because his gut told him to do it. But it was his head that made the final decision, with the advice of two key consultants.

The first was veteran scout Bill Killefer that Veeck had quietly assigned to follow Doby when he was with the Newark Eagles. The second was Wendell Smith, the sports columnist at the *Pittsburgh Courier*, a major Black newspaper. When the Dodgers signed Jackie Robinson, Smith was so close to the situation that he became Jackie's biographer and even roomed with him on the road. Veeck had done his homework. He knew the *Courier* was one of the leaders among Black newspapers from coast to coast, and sports was foremost among its readers because of writers like Smith.

Smith had seen Doby play many times and attested to both his skill and his off-the-field behavior. He told Veeck as much when he was asked for an educated opinion. Based on the feedback from his scout and Smith, Veeck purchased Doby's contract from the Eagles.

"I never knew the details," Mike Veeck told me, "but he was particularly proud that unlike Branch Rickey he had treated the Manleys [Abe and Effa], who owned the Eagles, with fairness in the negotiations. They had lost a great pitcher named Don Newcombe to Rickey and the Dodgers, who not only never paid them but didn't even bother to talk to them about it. That was racism of the worst kind.

"Years late, Dad conceded to me he was nervous because, as he later wrote, 'Cleveland wasn't Brooklyn.' But he believed his personal charisma and the city's love and respect for him could make it work. Almost from the beginning, the player he wanted was Larry Doby."

Another often overlooked factor facilitating Doby's later acceptance was the fact that, in 1946, the Cleveland Rams of the National Football League had moved to Los Angeles. In their place, a rebel league called the All-America Football Conference (AAFC) put a franchise in Cleveland.

Paul Brown, the team's popular coach, had no racial hangups. "I grade the films—I go by what I see," he said. Among the fan favorites were two Black superstars: fullback Marion Motley and offensive lineman Bill Willis, the latter known to the city as a standout middle guard at Ohio State.

To Cleveland's Black population, they were a welcome bonus because that same year, the Cleveland Buckeyes of the Negro American League folded. They were two-time Negro League World Series champions, but the ownership, sensing what was ahead for them in attendance after Robinson was signed that year, saw the future and believed, as Mrs. Manley did, that they were no longer in it. In their mind, there was no reason to fight a losing battle.

But Veeck was right. Much of the white population had its own "redneck" ideas refueled by Doby's arrival. Veeck announced he had received twenty thousand letters when he signed Doby. According to him, "Most were in violent and often obscene protest." He answered them all, "congratulating them on finding parents so obviously to their liking."

Doby spent the night he arrived in Chicago at a primarily Black hotel, the DuSable. He and Jones took a cab to the Congress Hotel, where the team stayed during its Chicago road trip, and picked up Veeck. As Veeck settled into the back seat, he put out his hand and said, "I'm Bill Veeck."

"Nice to meet you, Mr. Veeck," Doby said.

"Call me Bill," was the response.

When they reached Comiskey Park, Veeck signed a contract that would pay Doby $5,000 for the season plus a $1,000 bonus if he were still with the team after thirty days. Veeck also told him the dos and don'ts he'd face as a Black man in the American League.

Then he added something that shined a light between the midst of all the trauma and chaos that marked that first season and the hopes of the future. It became Doby's personal safety belt against his self-doubt, his manager's attitude, and the abuse and invective dealt upon him on the road.

It was Bill Veeck, the only voice that really counted, saying, "You are going to have problems and batting slumps—all players do. Believe me, I'll know, because I read box scores. You are going to have doubts—all players do. But when it gets toughest, I will fly to wherever the team is. We'll go to dinner and get the best steak in town and then we'll go out and hear the best jazz in town. And things will get better."

When he said that, Doby knew this was the start of a friendship that would endure. "He was color-blind," Larry often said. "He didn't see color. I always knew he was there for me."

"They respected each other," Mike added. "They agreed on almost everything." Laughing, Mike added, "Well, almost everything. Except music. Dad was a traditionalist. He loved Dixieland—Larry was into jazz like Wes Montgomery. I loved to hear them argue about it."

Years later, Doby would often take his son down to Eastern Shore, Maryland, to spend a few days with Veeck and son Mike. He told me about one really hot summer day when Bill said to Mike, "Hey, why don't you take him [Doby's son] down to the country club for a swim?"

When they left, Veeck looked at Doby, smiled, winked, and said, "Wait until the club members see the integrated package we just sent them. How long do you think it will take the folks down there to empty the pool?" What the kids did not know was that their fathers had spent the whole day planning it.

On the day Doby signed his contract, Veeck did and said the kinds of things that cemented their budding friendship. There was a press conference where Doby told the media, "Last night on the train was the first time I got to sleep since Mrs. Manley told me the Eagles had sold my contract. I'm really nervous."

Cleveland's baseball fans were more than willing to give him a chance. A man-in-the-street columnist produced the following conversation:

> *Question: "What do you think of Bill Veeck signing a Negro?" Answer from the fan: "Can he hit? That's all that matters, isn't it?"*

The answer was better than what most of his new teammates would give him.

Conversely, one Hall of Famer gave him nothing.

Rogers Hornsby, after watching Doby just once that year, made the following statement: "Bill Veeck did the Negro race no favor when he signed Larry Doby to a Cleveland contract. If Veeck wanted to demonstrate that the Negro has no place in Major League Baseball, he could have used no subtler means to establish the point. If he were white, he wouldn't be considered good enough to play with a semipro club."

Doby faced the moment as a stranger in a foreign land, and it was that way from when he joined the team up until the day game of the season. He was restrained and understood he was in a position where silence was not just golden—it was a matter of survival.

But later . . . after he became a hero and led the Indians to the American League pennant and then to the World Series championship . . . after he was a perennial All-Star and an MVP contender, and could speak up when the media unfairly challenged him . . . he made two statements so logical and overdue, it is a wonder that they didn't bury the folk myth forever.

First, he told *Jet* magazine, "Jackie [Robinson] got all the credit for putting up with the racists' crap and abuse. He was the first. But the crap I took was just as bad. Nobody said, 'We're going to be nice to the second Negro.'"

When asked, as he so often was, whether Robinson made it easier for him, he responded, "That's one of the stupidest questions I have ever been asked. Think about it. We're talking about weeks. Now it's fifty years later and you still have hidden racism among educated people. How could you change all that in just weeks?"

Branch Rickey dwelled so frequently on the achievement of, well, Branch Rickey during Robinson's first year, but Veeck was a polar opposite. After that first hastily called press conference on the field at Comiskey Park, Veeck made a point of publicly putting an arm around Doby's shoulder, smiling, and saying clearly, "Remember, Larry, they play the game up here with a little white ball and a stick of wood just like they did in your league." Then he left, after making sure the Cleveland writers learned that Larry was leading the Negro National League in both average and homers just before he joined the Indians.

And, true to his word, when times were plain awful, racism was a disgrace, and major-league curveballs were getting the best of him, Veeck was there no matter where the team was playing. The steaks and the jazz were good. The impact of Veeck's visits always made Doby feel a little better.

During homestands, he lived in Cleveland with an old Navy buddy, Arthur Grant. During World War II, they had been teammates on an all-Black segregated team called the Black Blue Jackets at Great Lakes Naval Training Station. When Doby joined the Indians, he moved into Grant's home.

But on the road, he was confined to Black hotels or boardinghouses where he knew no one and loneliness was his only companion. For the first time in his life, he was completely isolated. He was not only the first Black player on the Indians, playing for a team where arguably more than half the roster didn't even want him, but was also the only Black player among the more than three hundred whites in the entire American League.

On the road, cities like St. Louis and Washington were still segregated by Southern mentality. Doby often had to walk all the way to the stadium because there never seemed to be enough Blacks-only cabs to go around.

The worst were the fans at Sportsman's Park in St. Louis. For the rest of his life, he never forgot the rage that coursed through his entire body on a hot summer day there.

In fact, a vicious redneck almost forced him out of baseball completely.

The fan was standing in the first row, leaning over the railing. Below him, Doby was kneeling in the on-deck circle. He clearly heard the first salvo. "Nigger . . . nigger . . . nigger," it began. A refrain that was not new to him. Doby tuned it out.

"Yeah," he told me, "I could do that. I heard it often enough by then. But then he got far too personal. He started on my family."

"Yeah!" the fan screamed in a voice loud enough to shatter glass, "he is one uppity nigger—but if you think he's uppity, you should meet his wife. She spells her name H-e-l-y-n. But there wasn't anything uppity about her when you think about the things she did for me in my hotel room last night. She—" and then he followed with a disgusting scatological list.

He was vilifying the girl whose books Doby carried to Paterson Eastside High School. The girl he married when he signed his first Eagles contract. The woman with whom he consulted about every family decision since that day.

"That was it," Doby told me. "I ran straight for the railing and threw one leg over it. I really wanted to hurt him . . . but then I was suddenly flying backward through the air, hit the ground. Bill McKechnie, the coach who was one of just five who shook my hand the first day in the locker room, was on top of me.

"Don't move," he said. "Don't even think about going up there. Do it and you will never play another game of baseball anywhere. This is the American League. They don't like you. They don't like your skin color. Do it and we won't get another Black player in this league for ten years."

The event was more than a shocking footnote to a nightmare season. For the first time during a year of death threats, racism, and fan vitriol. Even speaking to me about it half a century later, Doby spoke with anger in his voice. As Mike Veeck said, "Larry Doby had been through so much. He could forgive, but never forget."

As a case in point, there was that angry memory of that first introduction to his Cleveland teammates.

One of the two players who not only did not shake his hand but turned to face the wall when Doby offered it was first baseman Eddie Robinson. On July 6, Doby's second day with the ballclub, the team had a doubleheader against the Chicago White Sox. Boudreau told him he was playing first base in the second game.

"Skip, I never played much first," Doby reminded him.

"Well, that's where I penciled you in," Boudreau said.

Doby walked across the locker room and asked Robinson to let him borrow his first baseman's glove.

"No," Robinson retorted angrily. "You can't." Then, according to Doby, he added a number of racial reasons why he couldn't.

Doby thought he might have to play first using his fielder's glove, but the Indians' traveling secretary walked to the White Sox dugout and borrowed a first baseman's mitt for him.

Decades later, on July 19, 1982, a retired Doby was invited to play in the in the inaugural Cracker Jack Old-Timers Baseball Classic. He took Larry Jr. with him.

Larry Jr. told me, "I knew Mickey Vernon, who had been an All-Star with the Senators, was stationed with dad in the Pacific and had written a letter to Clark Griffith, the owner, pointing out that although he was Black, the team should sign him. He got a nasty letter back telling him to mind his own business.

"Here was a guy who risked his own future to help my dad. I wanted to find him and thank him after the game. I was standing in the hotel lobby when I saw a man I was sure was him. So I walked over, put out my hand, and said, 'Mr. Vernon, I just want to thank you for what you tried to do for my dad—' and then I felt somebody yank me by my shoulder.

"It was my dad. He never looked at the guy I thought was Mickey Vernon. All he said was that it was time to go."

The man whose hand Junior tried to shake was actually that of Eddie Robinson.

As Doby had learned—going all the way back to his birthplace of Camden, South Carolina—there are some things you do not forget and some things you can never forgive.

CHAPTER 2

A JIM CROW SPRING BECOMES A HERO'S AUTUMN

Bill McKechnie's warning on the last day of the 1947 season was a stone in Doby's shoe. By the first snowfall of a Paterson winter, it had morphed into an emotional boulder.

The coach had told Doby, "I know you can and will hit. You have the perfect power hitter's swing—but we will never know if you don't get in the game. You are listed as an infielder. The manager plays shortstop. The second baseman is a perennial All-Star. And you didn't hit .200. So where do you fit?

"Listen to me. You go home and learn how to play the outfield. We are hurtin' there. Boudreau will have to give you a shot."

It was the second time McKechnie had saved his career, with the first being when he held him back from going after a heckler in St. Louis.

But how do you learn to play the outfield over the course of a single Paterson winter? Obviously, the North Jersey weather in no way duplicates a Miami day at beach. McKechnie never made his suggestion public. The only other baseball man with the same thought was hardly a source to whom Major League Baseball would pay the slightest attention.

Biz Mackey, a catcher and playing manager with the Negro National League Newark Eagles, had himself been shut out of all-white baseball. His Negro Leagues career lasted 30 years. At age fifty-two, still playing and managing, he was the Negro National League catcher of record in the All-Star Game. In 1946, he played and managed the Eagles to the Negro League World Series title. The second baseman on that team was Larry Doby.

Mackey had seen enough of Doby to stamp him as a future star when he integrated the Cleveland Indians.

"He can make it if the Indians are smart enough to play him in the outfield," Mackey said. "We know he can hit. He led our league in home runs and batting average on the day he left Newark to join the Indians. His numbers with the Eagles were fantastic. He has the speed of a major-league outfielder. I have no doubts he will deliver big if they give him an honest shot."

When you talk about hitters like Ted Williams and Rogers Hornsby, or outfielders like Willie Mays and Joe DiMaggio, you are talking about baseball's 24-karat gold-standard outfielder. In Doby, you are talking about a player whom Bill Veeck was sure would one day be part of both of those conversations. But in the winter of 1948, you were talking about a twenty-three-year-old prospect who seemed light years away from such comparisons.

But Mackey and McKechnie both knew that spring training of 1948 could well be his trial by fire. As the great boxing trainer Ray Arcel once said about how far raw determination can drive a fighter, "Tough times make guys with blue collars eat red peppers."

Larry Doby was a fighter, through and through. Whatever it took, he was willing to do. He needed to find a way to fulfill the prophecy of those old baseball lifers who had seen in him what his own big-league manager had not.

In preparation, he went to the Patterson library and checked out the book *The Way to Better Baseball* by then-Yankees right fielder Tommy Henrich. He fielded fungoes in the same public park where he had played during a remarkable high school career in which he learned eleven varsity letters. The training wouldn't be enough to make him a star, but it was a start.

Staying in physical shape during the off-season was no problem. He had been an exceptional high school basketball player; he joined the Paterson Crescents of the American Basketball League that winter and broke yet a second color line as the league's first Black player. At the other end of the spectrum, he also played for the New York Rens, an all-Black team that was named after the Renaissance Ballroom, a Harlem landmark.

Doby left for the Indians' Tucson, Arizona, spring-training camp in February 1948 not knowing how or if Boudreau would react when he offered to play the outfield. In a sport whose players are judged more by statistics than by potential, his manager had already given him little chance to prove himself. As noted, Doby had been leading the Negro National League in batting average and home runs when he left to join the Indians in July 1947. Despite those numbers, Boudreau was clearly skeptical. So

Doby was inserted mainly as a pinch-runner or pinch-hitter in 29 games, and received just 33 plate appearances. Small wonder that against those limitations he hit a miserable .156.

Veeck had planned the rookie debut for late in the 1947 season rather than send him to the minors for a year, just as the Dodgers had done with Jackie Robinson. Veeck knew that Doby was a player of serious potential, but also was keenly aware that Boudreau did not share his enthusiasm. Some in the front office even tried to persuade Veeck to release Doby outright or send him down to the minors for more seasoning.

Veeck was probably the most colorful and loquacious team owner in the history of the major leagues. But few realized that when the occasion warranted; he could be as secretive as a Navy SEAL. A case in point was the way he hid 3-foot-7 Eddie Gaedel from the media for a week and then stunned all of baseball by sending him to bat just once, resulting in a photo in which Detroit catcher Bob Swift, on his knees, towered over Gaedel. Veeck's silence produced a newspaper picture for the ages.

In 1947, while Doby was struggling for survival, Veeck signed Hall of Famer Tris Speaker to be what he called the Indians' goodwill ambassador. It was either a stroke of pure genius or the residue of blind luck. Either way, it produced a result straight out of Central Casting: the major-league making of Lawrence Eugene Doby.

For 22 seasons, Speaker dominated the American League. His lifetime batting average, playing for Boston, Cleveland, Washington, and Philadelphia, was an astonishing .345. He had 3,514 hits. But defensively, Speaker holds career records for unassisted double plays by an outfielder. His fielding glove was known as the place "where triples go to die."

After his playing and managing days, Speaker went into business. Ten years before he joined the Indians, he opened a wholesale liquor business. By the time Veeck brought him back to the game as a ceremonial ambassador, it was clear that Doby's immediate future was in serious danger with everyone in the organization. The front office formed a solid block of doubters.

"But I don't believe my dad ever considered their thoughts," Mike Veeck told me. "He was sure Larry would make it. As far as I know, dad never considered he wouldn't."

Everything Bill Veeck ever achieved in baseball was correctly tied to three factors: trust your instincts; pay attention to the people who buy the tickets; and there is no such thing as coincidence. If you doubt the last, then you are doomed not to see the forest through the trees. Maybe it was why he signed Speaker or, more likely, that he had something very different in mind when he did. I personally believe that Doby's struggle to find a position was the real reason he had signed Speaker the first place.

Veeck kept his public silence and quietly asked Speaker to take Larry Doby to school. He wanted—even needed—for Speaker to take this unproven neophyte, an infielder all his baseball life, and teach him all the nuances and tools needed to turn him into far more than an just average outfielder. At stake was Doby's career and an affirmation of Veeck's judgement that talent, not race, made a major-league player.

Only Veeck the visionary could have ignored so many apparent negatives and come away with the perfect "baseball odd couple."

Here was Doby, a twenty-four-year-old pupil, just months removed from a self-imposed exile to a space at the far end of the dugout, as distant from his manager as the bench would allow . . . a lonely Black man, unwanted by most opponents and many of his own teammates, in what then was a league whiter than a fresh Scandinavian snowfall . . . a gifted ballplayer so isolated by Jim Crow and racial stereotypes that his relationship with most of his teammates ended immediately after the final pitch was thrown.

And here was Tris Speaker, the sixty-year-old teacher, born and raised in the rabid-racist atmosphere of Hubbard, Texas, who never in his career played with or against a Black player, a man who allegedly had spent time in his youth as a member of the Ku Klux Klan and now was coupled with a Black man, thirty-six years his junior, in order to teach him how to play the outfield.

As different as they were in age, skin color, and background, how could Veeck think this could possibly work?

It worked because Veeck knew people and quietly understood that such a pairing could succeed because of Doby's determination to learn and Veeck's understanding that Speaker's subliminal motive was to dispel any reference to his earlier KKK experience. When he met Doby, he immediately shed the role of yesterday's hero and became the teacher who accepted today's challenge. Everyone knew Speaker was a brilliant player, a runner who once stole 52 bases in a season, and a hitter who set a big-league record with 792 doubles (a record that stands to this day).

But, given a fair chance, nobody needed to teach Doby how to hit. It was Speaker's defensive brilliance that made him Doby's perfect mentor.

The green expanse of the outfield at Tucson's Randolph Municipal Baseball Park (now Hi Corbett Field) became their daily classroom. It also helped that the outfield dimensions of Hi Corbett Field were larger than that of Municipal Stadium, which made it not only a great place to learn the position, but also to prepare him for an outfield that would be smaller than his home field (as he had learned in a larger outfield, making his home field easier to manage).

Doby wasn't the first aspiring outfielder to learn his skill there. Built in 1927, it was called home by three minor-league teams. The year before Veeck signed Doby, the Indians moved in. In 1948, Speaker ran a spring course there for Doby in "Outfield 101." It was a hell of a lot more than just catching fly balls.

As a young player early in his career with the Red Sox, Speaker was the leader in what was called the "Million-Dollar Outfield." After he was traded to Cleveland, Duffy Lewis and Harry Hooper, the two remaining Boston outfielders, admitted they had learned how to play specific hitters by asking and watching Speaker. Doby once said he learned something every day from Speaker.

Becoming a great outfielder—and Speaker made Doby one—requires agility, judgment, and a cannon for an arm. As the Yankees' Tommy Henrich once postulated, "Catching fly balls is fun. But what you do after you catch it, that's strictly business." That is the catechism that defines a great outfielder, and every skill Doby learned in Tris Speaker's classroom made him a star. In his playing days, Speaker was the best defensive outfielder in the majors. His prestige was so high that Ogden Nash, the king of the short poem, once penned this ditty in his honor:

S is for Speaker,
Swift centerfield tender,
When the ball saw him coming,
It yelled, "I surrender."

But the big link between teacher and pupil, and the reason for what evolved from it, was that they exchanged unexpected revelations about their own backgrounds. With a different teacher and a different student of the same shared backgrounds, that probably would not have worked. But in their learning about each other, this one turned into a genuine friendship—a Veeck specialty, as he had the skill of taking people from differing backgrounds with similar goals, and bringing them together to form unlikely bond.

Before year's end, Speaker had turned Doby into a superb defensive outfielder (first in right field and then in center, where he spent the majority of his time in Cleveland) and a key player in the Indians' first World Series winner since 1920. Relieved of what could have been a totally new defensive burden, Doby began to hit just the way he had with the Newark Eagles. During spring training in 1949, a year later, Speaker told *Washington Post* columnist Shirley Povich that he had "never seen a young ballplayer with such high potential."

Doby was ready for a breakout season, but there was an enormous gap between the on-the-field lessons Speaker taught him and his first spring training. Doby had joined the Indians on July 5, 1947. He had not been with the team during spring training, and for the first Black man in the American League, the Indians' trip to Cleveland was even more difficult and humiliating than playing in segregated St. Louis and Washington during the regular season.

The Indians and the New York Giants, whose spring home was in Phoenix, shared a train each year and played one another along the way. For the most part, the chain of cities in which they stopped and the minor-league parks in which they played formed a rednecked highway through the heartland of Jim Crow.

Doby did not discuss with his children the pain and humiliation of those first few spring trips, but Helyn knew. Because he did not live with his teammates, he had to reach those ballparks on his own, often walking because white cab drivers would not stop for him. Twice, racist security guarding the players entrances kept him out until Indians officials interceded.

In a rare conversation about those early springs, Larry Jr. recalled his dad once telling him about a Southern stop where the outfield fans bombarded him with full beer cans and garbage. Halfway through the game, he walked off the field.

"He told me the other half of the story fifty years later—the day before he was inducted into the Baseball Hall of Fame in Cooperstown, New York," Larry Jr. said. "We were sitting in the coffee shop at the Otesaga Hotel.

"'I think it was Columbus, Georgia,' he said. 'After the game, as I was leaving the clubhouse, I was approached by a well-dressed Black man. I don't remember his first name after all these years, but his last one was Alexander.

"'Mr. Doby, I am my town's only Black doctor. My wife and I think it is a disgrace that you have to live alone in a Black rooming house when the Indians play here. We want you to stay with us each time.'

"'They took me in three times. They treated me as family. Then, about ten years later, he went down to join a lunch-counter sit-in at J. J. Newberry and they killed him. A man like that? What was his crime? You tell me.'

"You should tell that story in your induction speech tomorrow," I said.

"It's the wrong time. I want to talk about the progress baseball has made since then. I want to talk about the progress we still need to make."

And he did.

The spring of 1948 would never fully be in his rearview mirror. It was another obstacle that helped shape him. During those early exhibition tours, he was alone for two springs, dressing in his hotel, unable to flag down taxis, often walking down the street in uniform all the way to the ballpark.

Back in Cleveland for homestands was a welcome change for him. Arthur Grant, his teammate on the Black Blue Jackets team in basic training, eventually got discharged and settled in Cleveland. Doby continued to live at his home, as did Helyn and the kids when they came to visit. But until July 7, 1948, when Satchel Paige joined the Indians, Doby remained a man alone on the road.

The spring games in Arizona in 1948 began with an invigorated Doby hitting well and playing the outfield with reasonable skill. But Speaker had no magic wand to wave and anoint Doby as a genuine outfielder. That had to be learned and earned: how to play a specific hitter; when to hit the cutoff man; when and where to throw in dozens of situations. And more: when to trust your arm and when to know its limitations. That spring, he was moved around the outfield—Boudreau was unsure what to do with him. But Speaker had seen enough to know exactly where he belonged.

On Opening Day, the center fielder was Thurman Tucker, who was obtained during the offseason in a trade with the White Sox for catcher Ralph Weigel (and who the Indians told the *Telegraph Herald* was "the finest defensive player in baseball"). Doby played right field and continued to hone his newly learned craft. In June, when Tucker broke a finger, Doby was moved to center. He played there as though he'd had the job for a decade. Score one for the Speaker-Veeck cabal.

There was one other personal factor that served as an unspoken spur to Doby. Washington and St. Louis were still segregated cities—Washington in particular a motivation to him, since he'd played there for the Eagles. The Black fans remembered him. They of course sat in a segregated section behind the outfield when Doby first played there. Each time he trotted back to his position, they gave him a standing ovation.

Collectively, they were his fans. Years later, when we discussed what Washington and St. Louis meant to him, he would smile and recall what seemed like an ocean of Black faces, bracketed by the rest of the seats and the boxes where they were not allowed to sit. The faces in the preferred seats were always whiter than the baseball. When we spoke about this, it seemed to trigger memories of the protective wall that fans who looked like him always offered up. It was as though they were saying, "We are here. Make us sit wherever you want, but we ain't going away. You can sit us in the worst seats and make us come in through the back door. Swing that bat, Larry, and remind them it is our game too."

Doby told me, "I always hit well in Washington and St. Louis. I saw them out in the Jim Crow seats. I felt like a high school quarterback with his own five thousand cheerleaders. I knew who was making the noise and exactly where it was coming from. And I will tell you they made some noise. When I hit a home run, their sound was deafening."

In his Hall of Fame acceptance speech in 1998, Larry said, "You know, most of them had never even been to a major-league park except for a Negro League game. They were nervous, and some of them couldn't afford it. But I knew why they came and why they were there. This Hall of Fame honor belongs to them."

On May 8, 1948, in Washington's Griffith Stadium, Doby for the first time gave them what they wanted: He hit his first home run in a segregated park. I wasn't there when it happened, but years later I got a phone call that put me there. I was at that induction ceremony and covered it for my paper. The man on the phone was John Thompson Sr., the former Georgetown basketball coach.

"I was one of those faces you wrote about," he said. "I was just a kid, but my dad took me there every time he came to town. We were an American League city, and he was the only reason we were there at that ballpark. He was our guy. Just to see him and applaud him each time he trotted out to his position in center field—everybody in those seats loved him. And when Satchel Paige joined the Indians that summer, it doubled our joy."

For the record, Clark Griffith, who owned the Senators and whose ballpark bore his name, made it clear how he felt about Black players.

Sam Lacy was the respected sports editor of the newspaper chain known as the *African-American*. He was raised within walking distance of the Senators' ballpark. As a kid he hung out there during summer vacations and ran errands for the players.

When he joined the newspaper chain, Griffith gave him a press pass. One day Lacy asked him, "Mr. Griffith, isn't it time you signed a Black player?"

"Sam, I can't do that. What would happen to the Black leagues? Think of all the unemployed colored men I'd create."

"I don't think they would worry about that," Lacy replied. "They didn't complain when Mr. Lincoln put more of us out of work when he signed the Emancipation Proclamation."

Griffith walked away.

When I told Doby that story, he smiled and said, "I wonder what he thought when I hit my home runs there."

On July 7 of that year, a year and two days after Veeck signed Doby, he signed forty-seven-year-old pitcher Satchel Paige. The other owners weren't impressed: "At forty-seven, what the hell is he gonna do for the Indians?" . . . "This ain't Black baseball." . . . "Yeah, he'll maybe put a few thousand asses in the seats, but that's about all."

But the truth was that nobody ever played in more games in more ballparks than Satch. The first time he ever threw a baseball was at the Mount Meigs Industrial School for Negro Children—an Alabama reform school. Before his career ended, researchers at the Baseball Hall of Fame figured that he pitched in more than 2,500 games and won about 2,000 of them, including 300 shutouts and 55 no-hitters. The critics were wrong. Whatever his age, he would leave a lasting impact on a rare Cleveland championship year. What could he contribute? What might he bring to the Indians that they lacked? Something the team would desperately need: a vanity-based arrogance that bred self-confidence.

His oft-quoted reason for his extended success was typical: "Work like you don't need the money. Love like you've never been hurt. Dance like nobody is watching. And don't look back, because somebody might be gaining on you."

Coming out of spring training in 1948, the Indians were not considered a major threat to the dominance of the world champion Yankees. Cleveland had three pitchers who were proven winners: Bob Feller, Bob Lemon, and Steve Gromek. A fourth pitcher, journeyman Gene Bearden, was still very much an unknown. For the most part, they were essentially the same team that finished fourth in the American League—17 games behind the first-place Yankees—the previous season. Cleveland had not won a pennant since 1920. Nobody expected much. Moreover, Bob Feller, the great fireballer, would have what for him was a so-so year.

During the preseason, the Yankees were the writers' and managers' choice to repeat as champions. The Red Sox were a heavy favorite to finish second. The Indians got just one vote predicting they could win a title. After the Yanks beat the Sox, 7–0, on June 29, Yanks manager Bucky Harris proudly predicted his then-second-place team would win the pennant. But in July, Cleveland was in surprising pursuit of the American League title, and more surprising was that the team they were wrestling with was not the Yankees but the Red Sox.

Harris never realized that there was another challenger in the game. Everyone knew that the Indians had pitching, but their supporting cast seemed to get overlooked—until they signed the one pitcher who was older and far more traveled than anyone on their staff. It was Satchel Paige, the man who threw a strange assortment of pitches and that everyone thought was brought in as a publicity stunt (which was a Veeck specialty). Two days after his signing, on July 9, Paige entered his first major-league game in the fifth inning in relief of Bob Lemon, who was losing to the Browns, 4–1. Paige gave up a single to Chuck Stevens, who was bunted over to second by Jerry Priddy. That brought up Whitey Platt, and the baseball world got to see firsthand what every Negro Leaguer had known about for decades: the wonder that was Ol' Satch.

He threw an underhand strike, then a sidearm strike. Then, finally, for the first time anywhere in a big-league game, came Satchel Paige's signature "hesitation pitch." A strange windup that seemed to take forever until it was even with the side of Satch's head, poised there frozen in time, and suddenly fired toward home plate. It fooled Platt so much that he threw his bat forty feet down the third-base line. The Browns dugout screamed "Balk! Balk!" in unison. All the umpire yelled was "Strike three!" A fly ball off the bat of Al Zarilla ended the inning. A popup and a double play ended the next. The Browns won, but nobody ever considered Paige a publicity stunt again. Then on August 3, a record 72,562 fans saw him beat the Senators, notching his second career victory. And just like that, Boudreau suddenly had more pitching than any manager in the American League.

Now there were two Black men on the Indians—the only two in the American League. Segregation remained, but Doby had his first big-league roommate on the road.

Asked what that was like, Doby would betray no emotion except to say with a straight face, "I don't know. I was rooming with a suitcase."

They were teammates, not friends. Doby respected Paige's ability to stand up for his record Negro League paychecks, his extracurricular semipro earnings that his Negro League teams tolerated, and the fact that his addition to the roster helped all of them make more money. He respected what Satch could do with a body (and arm) that was nearly a half century old.

But he was not in any other way a fan of the image Paige projected in the locker room and during media interviews. On the surface, both were equally proud men. Paige was fiercely prideful of his astounding baseball achievements, as was Larry of being his own man—not trying to draw attention to what kind of Black man others wanted him to be.

The difference was that Satchel always gave them the stereotypical *Amos 'n' Andy* shuffling image he thought they wanted—which most of them did. If that was what they wanted, he was willing to play the clown.

Larry hated that image. And he hated even more the way Satch was more than willing to portray it for them. Amos and Andy to him were symbols of a time that should be relegated forever to America's rearview mirror. To Satch, it made no difference. He was a give-'em-what-they-want kind of guy.

The season, meanwhile, ticked away with surprising moments. Even the Philadelphia Athletics made a futile visit to first place, but on the last day of the season the Indians and the Red Sox were dead even with 96 victories.

The pitcher Boudreau sent into the one-game playoff was the one with the shortest résumé. Gene Bearden, a wounded war hero with a dead-fish knuckleball that had no speed and no consistent direction, would be the surprising standard-bearer on just two days' rest. Boudreau, who was on his way to the MVP Award at shortstop, was playing a hunch that would make him a managerial genius.

Against him, Red Sox manager Joe McCarthy attempted a gamble of his own. Thinking ahead to the World Series, he chose to save 15-game winner Mel Parnell, who had beaten the Indians three times that season, and instead gave the ball to Denny Galehouse (who was 8–7 on the season).

Galehouse was no match for the Indians' hitters, giving up four runs in just three innings. Bearden, on the other hand pitched a complete-game five-hitter, and Cleveland won handily, 8–2. Boudreau himself hit not one but two home runs.

The Indians came into the Series loaded with pitching. They had depth and quality. Against that, the Boston Braves staff had amazing quality of its own. Left-hander Warren Spahn and right-hander Johnny Sain were the best duo in baseball. But two arms were not a fair match against the volume of the Indians' side.

A popular limerick had been the Braves' battle cry at Braves Field all season long: "Spahn and Sain and pray for rain."

It might have been enough in a short series, but the sky stayed cloudless and clear. Against the power lodged within the Indians batting order, the pitching duo was not enough.

That set the stage for the Braves and National League fans to discover that Jackie Robinson was not the only Black man in baseball.

It was, for all intents and purposes, a coming-out party for Larry Eugene Doby.

He became the first African American to hit a home run in a World Series game. In the Series, Doby hit at a .318 clip as the most prolific Indian, with seven hits in 22 at-bats and a .500 slugging percentage. The Indians won in six games, and it's remembered not as the end of a near-three-decade championship drought but as a moment in time when an alert photographer snapped one of the most significant photographs of the civil-rights era. It has endured as the beginning of the end of the racial discrimination in baseball that had lasted more than a century.

He was a staff photographer with the *Cleveland Plain Dealer.* The Indians had just won Game Four, the game in which Larry Doby hit his historic home run. Steve Gromek was standing in a corner of the room when he looked past the celebration and spotted Doby. "Tell him to come over for a picture," the photog said. Gromek motioned to Larry, who crossed the room and threw his left arm around Gromek's right shoulder. Gromek hugged Doby with his own left. They faced the camera with a set of smiles brighter than the aurora borealis.

It wasn't a staged reaction. What it was instead was a reflection of spontaneous joy. A year earlier, Gromek was one of five players who shook Doby's hand when he first integrated the Indians dressing room. The expressions on their faces captured more than the thrill of victory.

Doby said it best: "That was a feeling from within, the human side of two people. One Black. One white. That made up for everything I went through. I would always relate back to that whenever I was insulted or rejected from hotels. I would always think about that picture. It would take away all the negatives."

In an interview with *The Athletic*, Larry Jr. spoke about the photo, saying That was probably the most special moment in his career. . . . It was just two guys who were expressing an unbridled joy over accomplishing a common goal. I think that picture really encapsulates what that journey and the hardships meant to him."

Just as Doby rarely discussed with his son what he had gone through, so it was with Steve Gromek and his sons. One of them, Greg, recalled that it wasn't until they were older that he told them.

It is more than nine hours by car between Doby's home in Paterson, New Jersey, and Gromek's in Hamtramck, Michigan. "When I got home," Doby told friends and interviewers in Paterson, "that picture represented for me the happiest day of my life."

Ironically, there were people in Michigan who told Steve Gromek, "You could have shaken hands with him—you didn't have to hug the colored guy." One of them was an old friend with whom he had played ball. Gromek never spoke to him again.

There were even death threats. But Gromek never saw color. He was delighted to repeat a local story that may have been apocryphal. It was alleged that a female parishioner complained about the photo to her parish priest. "If someone won a World Series game for me," the priest was said to have responded, "I'd have done more than hug him."

But neither the priest nor Steve Gromek knew the photo was a precursor to a new day in baseball. It was a graphic representation of a future that America should have celebrated.

It appeared on the front pages of newspapers across the country—even in the South, where a Black man and a white man had never shared their common joy in as prominent a setting as that.

"I must have walked past that photo a hundred times in the den, where my dad kept his baseball memorabilia," Greg Gromek told me. "Both of them signed it. I'd routinely walk past it most days when I was a kid. But it wasn't until I was older that I understood how much it meant to my dad and to Mr. Doby, and, finally, I guess to America."

Doby and I talked about the iconic picture only once. I remember saying to him, "It's the faces, Larry, the faces. The two of you look as though you are sharing a great secret that only the two of you know."

Who is to say they weren't?

It was also a photo that a good slice of America was not willing to share. It was taken before the Warren Supreme Court outlawed school segregation . . . before Rosa Parks refused to move to the back of the bus . . . before Dr. Martin Luther King Jr. played a pivotal role in the Montgomery bus boycott that her action inspired . . . even before President Lyndon Johnson signed the 1964 Civil Rights Act, and before "Bloody Sunday" in Selma on the Edmund Pettis Bridge.

Doby spoke of the photo at his Hall of Fame induction in 1998, pointing out, "Back then, America and baseball needed that photo. And I am proud that I could be one of the two men who gave it to them."

Not everybody understood. When he tried to buy a home in an exclusive Paterson neighborhood a month after the 1948 World Series, he was legally denied by a codicil in the homeowners association by-laws that limited sales to "White Christians" only.

Meanwhile, the picture grew both in impact and stature. It deservedly reached a status far beyond the two families and far beyond the positive scrutiny of historians of baseball and America.

Doby and Gromek have since passed away, yet their families have remained in casual touch. But fifteen years after Jackie Robinson was awarded the Congressional Gold Medal, a New Jersey congressman named Bill Pascrell spearheaded a drive that earned the Congressional Gold Medal for Larry Doby Sr.

Junior called the Gromeks on the phone to request their help. What is pictured on the reverse side of every such medal is a decision that's up to the recipient or the family. For Larry Doby Jr., there was no doubt about what belonged there: "the picture."

Underneath it is this quote, often told by Doby to his kids. He said it at his Baseball Hall of Fame induction as well. It cuts to the heart of the photo's message: "We are stronger together, as a team, as a nation, as a world."

Larry Jr. and the Gromeks had never met. Junior worked for the pop-rock star Billy Joel, who had been scheduled to perform in Detroit. Larry offered them tickets to the concert. Instead, they suggested he come to Hamtramck and meet the whole family. He was invited to dinner at the home of Carl Gromek, Steve's oldest son.

A lot of Gromeks were there to greet him. They met as total strangers, but the dinner, according to Greg Gromek, was special to everyone. There wasn't an awkward moment for anyone. "It was as though we had known him for decades," Greg said. Steve's ninety-eight-year-old widow went out of her way to express her joy for the entire Doby family.

"Before long I realized that this family felt the same way about the picture that I did," Greg added. "We had a shared memory for so long, but we didn't understand it until we got older. Sitting together at dinner, we realized that what had once been an old photo on the wall of dad's den had become a family heirloom and, finally, something iconic of historical significance for the whole world.

"When we took pictures, we reenacted the photo with our arms around each other just like our dads did."

He was right, of course. Larry Sr. himself would never view it as I do. He was far too much of a gentleman for that.

Things being what they were at the time, however, I have my own opinion: I prefer to think of it as a justifiable middle-finger salute aimed directly at Judge Kenesaw Landis's failed racist battle to keep what he called "his game" whiter than a Grandma Moses snowfall.

CHAPTER 3

CAMDEN, SOUTH CAROLINA, AND THE LIVIN' WAS EASY—IF YOU WERE WHITE

The Civil War was over. On April 2, 1865, General Robert E. Lee surrendered at Appomattox, Virginia, and a week later the Confederate States of America ceased to exist. The newly freed South Carolina Blacks looked forward to a new day. South Carolina white plantation owners looked for a way to keep what they'd had under the old one.

Hanging over both sides was the intent of a document signed by Union General William Tecumseh Sherman, three months before hostilities ended. It granted 400,000 acres of Confederate land to freed slaves. Colloquially it was called "40 acres and a mule."

In January 1866, mixed crowds from both groups gathered in front of the Camden courthouse to hear the local commander of Union troops speak. He reminded them Lincoln was dead, and so was Sherman's promise. The new president was Andrew Johnson, who had absolutely no intention of honoring those commitments.

The terror of the Ku Klux Klan, founded two years later throughout the South by Confederate General Nathan Bedford Forrest, was rife in the state and, combined with the oppressive economics of the sharecropper system, now dominated the South. It would have a long, arrogant, and often violent run. By 1917, segregation effectively ruled the South.

It ruled Camden as well. Only two industries brought a kind of economic independence to a segment of the local Black population beyond the indentured servitude of life as a sharecropper: hotels and horses.

The former was racist by design in its advertising. It fed off Northerners' misconceptions of Southern hospitality. It created a kind of mythical appeal to the kind of "Old South" that existed only in the fantasy that grifters fed to potential Northern tourists. It recreated the pre-slavery idea of easy living resorts with all-Black staffs catering to everything white tourists needed. Ironically, it did employ a lot of Black men and women.

Horses were something else. A plethora of showhorses, steeplechasers, and even thoroughbreds were sent South to Camden for winter training and events. Soon, polo horses joined the growing field. Based on the tourist trade, the Kirkwood Hotel immediately built a polo field on its land that attracted wealthy polo horse owners and enthusiasts. The weather was good, and stable help provided by a young Black population was plentiful and dependable.

Horses had become serious business in Camden, not only for steady local Black employment but also after the local season, when much of the stable staff traveled North with those same horses to the established tracks for their seasons. One of those grooms was David Doby.

David was a familiar figure around the Kirkwood polo stables, both due to his skill with horses and his growing reputation within the Black community as a power-hitting first baseman with the Camden Sluggers, a semipro team that was the best in all of South Carolina's Black baseball circles.

And it was baseball itself that gave David Doby a separate universe in which to escape—if only for nine innings—from the burden of being a Black man pressured by a white world. Except for a grateful trainer or two, he and his peers got little if any respect at the track. Even paying Black spectators at the Springdale Racecourse on Carolina Cup race day were segregated behind a special fence to view the races.

But at American Legion Stadium in his Camden Sluggers uniform, Doby was judged by the purest of standards. Could he hit the curve? Could he stretch for an errant throw and dig it out of the dirt with the dexterity to turn a potential infield hit into a routine out? A baseball-savvy crowd knew he could do both, and then some. On the playing field, without a white man in either team's uniform, skin color meant absolutely nothing. He knew it was there that he was the sole master of his fate.

David married a local girl named Etta Barnes, and for a time they lived with her parents on Market Street. Their son, Larry, was born on December 13, 1923. David started him playing baseball when he was seven, but the father's time with his son was limited.

David was a typical Camden stable hand. He would split each year between Camden and the tracks up North, sending money home for his family.

His long hours, his baseball, and his time on the road as a traveling groom put tremendous stress on his marriage with Etta.

Looking back, locals remembered his consistent baseball ability. But more than that, they remembered Larry as the little boy following his dad, carrying a worn old baseball glove wherever they went.

When Larry was around six years of age, his dad was up in Saratoga with the horses. On his day off, David Doby decided to go fishing. For reasons unclear, he fell overboard and drowned. He was just thirty-seven years old when he left Etta a widow.

There was a family meeting. Etta logically felt her best shot at supporting her son was as a domestic in the North, where salaries for such jobs were far better than those in Camden. It was decided that she would travel to New Jersey to seek employment, while her son would remain in Camden with his maternal grandmother, Augusta, until she could send for him.

This was not an unusual arrangement in the South, and one that continued through World War II because the lure of factories and shipyards and other jobs with better paydays separated a lot of Black families. The hitch in Etta's plans arose when she found a good job with a family in Ridgewood, as a live-in domestic. But there were no live-in arrangements for her son. Except for summers in Paterson visiting his mother, he would need to remain in Camden with his grandmother throughout most of his preteen years.

It was the mores of Camden that shaped him—a Camden that dictated the "separate and non-equal" rules for a Black kid growing up in the South. Camden and Miss Augusta, who supervised his education, oversaw his chores and enforced the work ethic with which he grew. She also believed that Sunday was a day of rest and prayer—not in that order. Every Sunday they attended services at the local Methodist church.

Despite the racist rules still thrust upon the minorities of Camden, there were reasons they were better off economically than other South Carolina Blacks living elsewhere in isolation as sharecroppers or gathered in small communities where night riders, Klansmen, and racist police brutally enforced their laws—written and unwritten.

The reason economic enterprise took root in the success of a vibrant Camden Black community was that it thrived on its own without white competition or interference. Tourism and horses put money in the pockets of the residents of "Black Bottom" (as most of their community was called). Clustered around streets like DeKalb, Market, and Broad, Black merchants thrived. Servicing it were three funeral homes, Dibble & Brothers Grocery, the Whitaker Drug Store, the Central Barber Shop, and the medical office of Dr. Pickett, Camden's first Black doctor. Additionally, two cotton-processing plants owned by whites hired Blacks.

While Camden remained forcibly segregated, there was a large enough Black population to support its own business community. Still, in the case of young Larry Doby, it was his grandmother who made sure he knew what he could and could not do in any interaction with the lighter-skinned community.

Against that backdrop, Doby began his formal education at the all-Black Jackson public school. Despite segregation, and despite the death of his father and the absence of his mother, baseball and Miss Augusta brought a sense of stability to his youth. But his grandmother was not aging well. Finally, she suffered bouts of what was thought to be dementia, which necessitated another family meeting. Etta's married sister-in-law, Alice Cooke, and her husband, James, lived in Camden and agreed to take Larry into their home. For the third time in his young life, he was being raised by a strong Black woman.

The Cookes were not happy with Larry's educational progress at Jackson and immediately enrolled him at Mather Academy, a private school. Founded by a Methodist missionary, Mather Academy was the vision of Sarah Babcock Mather. She went to Camden in 1867 and opened a school for African American children. The overcrowded school was financed with her money, and Mather sought to establish a larger institution. She purchased twenty-seven acres near Camden to build the new school. Decades later, enrollment reached almost four hundred students when Doby entered in the third or fourth grade. It was there that Larry met Richard Dubose and fell in love with the game of baseball.

Horse racing and polo were sports of the white community. But on the Black side of town, the game for all ages was baseball—and Richard Dubose was their hero. His major role was as the manager of the Camden Sluggers, but he was also the Mather Academy baseball coach. It was Dubose who had developed David Doby as the star first baseman of the Sluggers. Dubose immediately wondered if this coincidence had handed him a case of "like father, like son."

It didn't take long for Dubose to find out.

He determined that young Doby would be a first baseman.

"The boy was just a natural player," Dubose once said. "If there ever was such a kid with that ability, it was him. When he was with me, I played him at first just like his daddy. To look at him was deceiving. He was such a skinny kid you'd never realize the power he had in those skinny arms until you saw him throw the ball or swing a bat. He just loved it. He immersed himself in baseball. When he was about twelve years old, I would sneak him onto the Sluggers' travel roster, and if we were way ahead or way behind so that the game was already decided, I would slip him in to play an inning or two. It didn't matter how much older the opposition was, he always performed. Young as he was, he played with us in many parts of the state. I knew that when he matured he would make it big somewhere."

When Larry did mature, the lessons of Camden were not forgotten: the decision of the Cookes to enroll him at Mather that had prepared him for the much tougher standards in a Paterson high school; the baseball basics he had learned from Dubose made him a superior player; and the down-home structure of Miss Augusta and the Cookes with which he was raised gave him a sense of dignity that carried him through the dark years of loneliness and racism that marked his American League debut.

Although he lived most of his life in Paterson and Montclair, at his induction to the National Baseball Hall of Fame, he began his six-minute speech with "I come from a small town in South Carolina named Camden."

The little boy with the battered old baseball glove never forgot his roots.

Larry's last two years at Mather were a kid's wonderland. The Cookes were sticklers for the rules, but they never let them interfere with the things that mattered to the young boy. Academically, to their relief, he represented no problems. Socially, he had friends. And above everything else there was baseball, learning under the apprenticeship of Richard Dubose.

Baseball opened new worlds. When Dubose would occasionally take him on the road with his senior team, it revealed a new universe of places like Columbia and Charleston that dwarfed the limitations of what he was used to on DeKalb or Market Street.

But during his final three summers at Mather, his mother sent for him to spend his summer vacations in Paterson. The experience catapulted him into an urban world and an inner-city life he never knew existed, a place where his athleticism immediately made for easy acceptance. He learned the street games of a new culture: stickball, boxball, kick the can. Of course, there was still plenty of baseball.

At the end of the second summer, he bid his new friends goodbye and said he would see them again next year. He did, but not in the way he expected. After he graduated from Mather, he was told that his mother wanted him full-time in Paterson for high school. She felt that as a young Black man staring at his future, he needed the educational advantages of the North. The conversation would trigger their first serious quarrel. No more Camden, no more baseball under Dubose, no more time with his close friends. For the first time in his young, structured life, he rebelled against authority.

He argued, debated, even cried. But Etta remained firm. In 1938, after a summer in Paterson, he entered Paterson Eastside High School. Etta was right about the educational advantages brought by the move. Eastside had been built just fifteen years earlier, and there was simply no comparison between its facilities and faculty—all far superior to those of Mather. The negative was that there were only about twenty-five Black students when he enrolled. Nevertheless, his brilliant athletic ability contributed to his popularity among other students.

Etta was still working as a live-in domestic in Ridgewood, but she had a large circle of female friends in Paterson, and Doby would live with several of them in the Carroll Street neighborhood, near Graham Avenue, seeing her on Thursdays (the traditional maids' day off). But the neighborhood was perfect for a kid up from the Deep South trying to make new friends.

And, once again, he would be raised by strong Black women. The area was heavily Jewish, but also had a number of Black families. Doby recalled he experienced little racism within the immediate bounds of the neighborhood as a teenager. But downtown, at movie houses like the Fabian or the Majestic, was another story.

Though now in the North, Blacks were still confined to the balcony. For Doby, however, the new neighborhood was the perfect venue given his adolescence with the rules and mores of Camden and the transition to his new lifestyle in Paterson. When he was a senior, a neighborhood kid named Joe Taub—a first-generation Jewish boy from Polish immigrants—was a freshman who was awestruck by the young man who was the best as well as the most versatile athlete in the school's 15-year history. As a case in point, it was Larry Doby who taught Taub to shoot a two-handed set shot in that pre-jump shot era. They were friends for life. Taub made his fortune as a founder of the payroll-management company ADP. After his time in big-league baseball, Doby would work for the Taub-owned New Jersey Nets of the National Basketball Association.

The neighborhood where Taub and Doby first met was deep in the heart of Paterson's Fourth Ward. It was home to Paterson Elementary School No. 6, and the town's first public library. Enough mom-and-pop stores dotted the area between Carroll and Hamilton so that residents could do all their shopping nearby. Everything from the obligatory kosher butcher to the bagel factory was within walking distance. The bagel shop was owned by the Cohens and was known to everyone as "Bake and Babe." The bakers they supervised were racially integrated, and the shop was about much more than bagels. To gain access you lined up in a long, nameless alley in the wee hours of Saturday morning. The line stretched around the block, and the wait was as much a block meeting and a place to trade neighborhood gossip as it was to shop. The line itself reflected the neighborhood, heavily Jewish but also racially mixed. The bagels were sixty cents a dozen.

On a sunny day in late June of 1997, at my request, Taub and Doby agreed to revisit Carroll Street and share memories of the way it was when Doby arrived in Paterson. It went like this.

They greeted each other at the intersection of Carroll and Harrison, remembering a time as adolescents at the dawn of the 1940s. They talked of FDR serving his third term as president, Duke Ellington jazzing his way up the music charts, and World War II being fought in Europe. Paterson was a thriving manufacturing town—blue collar, neighborly, and safe. The downtown movie houses were segregated, but the neighborhood shared by the duo was not. For Taub and Doby, that world seemed a simple place.

"We were two street kids who came from humble parents, just two poor kids in a mixed poor neighborhood," Taub said.

"Our neighborhood was different than the rest of the world," Doby added. "The rest of the world had problems. Our neighborhood did not."

They walked through a light drizzle, and at first glance you would think they had nothing in common. Taub's silk navy-blue business suit fit flawlessly and his Black leather loafers had been recently shined. Doby's style, like his mannerisms, was understated. He wore a windbreaker over a pair of Dockers and a Negro League baseball cap. Few people they see along the way are aware of who he was. But what these two shared as they walked along Carroll Street was history—a bond that will last for a lifetime.

"There is this gut feeling you get growing up here," Taub said. "Everyone was shrewd and looking for an angle. There was a hidden instinct you develop on this street. We knew we couldn't con each other. So we were honest. We trusted each other."

Through the years they shared many walks along Carroll. Taub, who passed away in 2017 at the age of eighty-eight, said coming back was his way of keeping grounded. Sometimes he and Doby would do it together. As they walked, they renewed old memories.

"The best days of my life were spent right here," Doby said.

But that world lived only in the back roads of their minds. The old neighborhood looked different now. Doby's former home was demolished years earlier, and Taub's four-story apartment house from his past was bruised with graffiti, both in English and Spanish. Fats Berliner's candy store was long gone. A public housing project had replaced the ground that used to be Newman's playground. Broken beer bottles and yesterday's fast-food boxes littered the sidewalks their mothers once swept clean.

On this day, the rain had kept most residents inside. Except for the sound of windshield wipers on the passing traffic and the shrieks of a woman who ordered her toddler to "get out of the goddamn car," Carroll Street was silent. Doby and Taub ignored the angry woman, and chose not to dwell on the urban decay as they walked. They were too busy resurrecting a world that used to be. Theirs was a friendship of more than sixty years.

One of Taub's fondest memories is of Doby—"the Mighty Dobes," as he called him—standing in the middle of Carroll Street hitting baseball-size rocks over the tenement roofs. "He would do that for hours," Taub recalled. "He would throw rocks up high and then smack 'em out of sight. He was three years older than me, and whatever game I saw him play, he was always my hero."

Taub was born in Paterson, the second son of Jewish parents Sylvia, a domestic, and Morris, a junk man. Doby could stand outside Joe's four-story apartment house at 4345 Carroll Street and easily hit one over the rooftop and down a block to the duplex where Doby and his mom lived. Not a day passed without fifteen or twenty boys in front of Fats Berliner's candy store, someone would toss a ball, and a stickball game would erupt.

"If you could strike out Dobes," Taub said, "you were the hero of the day. But that did not happen very often." He stopped walking so he can gesture during that comment.

The games would last until twilight. Then neighbors could see Doby throwing a ball back and forth against someone's front steps by the headlights of a neighbor's car. Doby was as skilled with a ball and stick as Taub was with money. Playing gin rummy in the back room of a local storefront, he'd turn dimes into dollars, and then treat the gang to a taxi ride through Manhattan to see the lights and the sights.

Doby said that Taub could always outthink and outhustle anyone in the neighborhood. What Doby didn't know was that later, after he became a fixture with the Indians, he was helping

Taub win yet another hustle. That was during the summer of 1949—Larry was belting the hell out of the ball during a fabulous hot streak, while Joe Taub and a guy named Joe Ruff were riffling the cards just as hard.

Ruff had been a local athletic hero, too, and Taub was out to break his concentration. Ruff would start to put some boxes on the score sheet, and Taub would just sit back and wait for the right moment.

"Hey, Larry went 4-for-4 today," Taub would say, reaching for a card.

"Huh," Ruff would grunt, failing to note the card Taub had pulled off the discard pile. "I can play better than that turkey." Then he'd pick up a card and in his distraction throw away a card Joe needed.

"He used to carry my bag to the park," Ruff would say.

"Yeah—by the way, that's gin," Taub responded, laying down his hand.

Doby was enterprising as well. He was what orthodox Jews call "a Shabbas goy": he would be paid ten cents on Saturdays to turn out the lights for several ultrareligious Jews among his neighbors. He'd spend his earnings on movies at the Majestic downtown. His friends would go with him, and when they got there they would separate, and he would climb the stairs to sit in the Black section.

But nothing like that ever happened on Carroll Street.

Doby stopped walking to make a point. "None of our parents talked Black or white at the supper table. And when you got in the street, you were a member of a team—not as Black or white but as a player.

"It was that background that helped a little when I stepped into the Indians' locker room the first time and I didn't exactly get a very warm greeting. I called Joe that night and told him, 'You know what? I guess I never knew what it was like to be Black.'" Taub laughed and said, "It never came up on Carroll Street."

Long before they met for this stroll down memory lane, Taub was in his basement shepherding an idea called ADP that would change the way business is done in this country; Doby, who used to hit rocks over the rooftops of Carroll Street, was just a furlong away from integrating the American League forever.

I will never forget that day—two boys grown older reliving the purity of Carroll Street.

"I followed him from the day he left for Cleveland," Taub said. "I read every box score. When he played in New York, I was there. When I saw him get picked off base, I didn't sleep for two nights. And when his home run helped the Indians win the 1948 World Series and Paterson threw a parade for him, I was there in the street with all his fans."

So why did they agree to retrace Carroll Street yet one more time?

Doby never hesitated. "You should never be allowed to forget the place that shaped you."

CHAPTER 4

LIFE IN THE BIG CITY: TOUCHDOWNS, HOME RUNS, AND FIRST LOVE

Back home in Camden, South Carolina, where baseball was the unchallenged king of all sports for Blacks and whites, David Doby's kid was more than just a work in progress. On the segregated playing fields and bleachers, they began to suspect that he wasn't just a promising prospect—he was the wunderkind of the future. His coach knew it, and that's why he would occasionally have his twelve-year-old playing with and against grown men.

Now it was autumn in Paterson, and the dawn of a vastly different world for the young Doby. It was his freshman year at Paterson Eastside High. It would be months before baseball, months before he would step into a batter's box. Before that, his athleticism would be bracketed between one hundred yards and twin goalposts, followed by the snows of winter, the steamy indoor gym, and the echo of the cheers as his two-handed set shot found nothing but net. And then a springtime of base hits.

By then, the word was out in scholastic circles. A freshman named Larry Eugene Doby was a force to be reckoned with no matter the sport. Perhaps nobody was more surprised than Larry himself. Just as he had been in that preschool Carroll Street neighborhood, Larry had become the athlete every boy wanted to be.

It started with football—a sport he had never played. As a freshman, he won a starting job as a pass-catching end, but after two years was moved to wide receiver so they could take more advantage of his speed.

His only living high school teammate, Al Kachadurian, was ninety-nine years old when I interviewed him in 2022. "Whoever told you that was right—he had terrific speed," Al remembered. "No matter what the sport, speed beats everything. His speed was amazing. I honestly think he could have made it in the NFL or the NBA. And we know he did in Major League Baseball."

In those high school days, I don't think Kachadurian had ever had a Black teammate before, and neither had any other athlete at Eastside. So the next question was obvious. How was Doby accepted? Kachadurian and he became co-captains of the team.

"I never even thought about it. I played football and baseball with him. I played semipro baseball against him. When I threw passes, he was generally the guy who caught them. There were no adjustments because he was Black. Why would there be? He was invited to every party the football team held. The girls were all white and they really liked him. He was our teammate. We had his back, and when they roughed him up, we were there for him. There were a lot of teams we had to prove that against. I remember that Passaic was the worst.

"But a funny thing about that was I never, ever heard him curse. They would punch him and kick him when he was at the bottom of a pileup. He'd get up and just look at them and walk away. And then he'd make a play and beat them with his legs. If it had been me, I would have had a lot to say. I would have used a lot of very bad words to say it. I think that was a reflection of the way he was raised. I think that's the way it was when he broke the American League color line at Cleveland. I don't think he ever said anything when they threw at him. He just went out and beat them with his bat."

Later, when he faced the pressure of being the first Black in the American League, skeptics said he was too moody. Did Kachadurian find any of that when racism was serious among opponents in his high school days and he kept silent?

"Once in a while he was moody. But he came up from the South, and I don't know what he saw down there. He was Black, so who knows? But I'd prefer to say he was more stoic. That's why he never said anything after they jumped him in a football pileup—after he got kicked or punched. There was nothing he could do anything about. It was more 'I can't beat the world with words, but I can beat it and win whatever game we were playing with talent.' I would call that stoic.

"I might have missed something, but I don't think I ever heard any of our own players say anything about his race back at Eastside. When his mother got sick for a while, my mother even did his laundry. I don't know what he felt deep down. I mean, we never talked about race. We talked about sports. But looking back, we were all athletes, and he was a great teammate."

This is the way his 1942 graduating class remembered his senior year:

> Football—Eastside upset Montclair on opening day. It took advantage of a blocked kick and Larry Doby scored the only touchdown in a 7–0 victory. It might

have been the first time Eastside ever beat Montclair. It finished the season with an 8–1 record and won the state championship in its group. In the traditional Thanksgiving Day game it defeated its crosstown rival Paterson Central, 45–6, in front of 12,000 people. Doby caught three touchdown passes, was named all-state and Eastside won the first state championship in the school's 15-year history.

Basketball—Doby was the captain for his last two years and the driving force in the overtime game that brought Eastside its second straight league title. Doby again made the all-state team. There were some scouts who actually believed he was better at basketball than baseball.

Baseball—He played both baseball and track at the same time his senior year. All-state in baseball and lettered in track, where he ran the 440. He participated on the high school baseball and track teams at the same time. Hit .400 in 1942 and .559 the previous season.

But Doby would say that it wasn't at Eastside but rather between Eastside seasons when he took his biggest baseball step since Camden and Coach Dubose. Like Dubose's Camden Sluggers, this team, the Smart Set, was managed by a man whose reputation was rooted in the Black community. His name was Pat Wilson. I had never heard of him, and Doby had never forgotten him. Larry brought up the name during one of those days when he was talking about his early years in baseball.

"Starting with Mr. Dubose," he wondered, "how many managers did I play for? I mean all of them, from the time I was a little kid in South Carolina until the day I retired."

"Who knows? Maybe thirty," I wondered out loud. "So who was the best?"

He smiled, paused. "Pat Wilson."

"All right, you got me. Who was Pat Wilson?"

"Like I said, the best manager and teacher I ever played under. I played for him during high school summers on a semipro team you never heard of: the Paterson Smart Set."

Doby was always reluctant to talk about the negatives he had to conquer on his journey toward acceptance, but when he did, the story was always worth the wait. This was in the 1940s. Paterson didn't have a professional team of its own, although Negro National League teams used to play at Hinchliffe Stadium up by the Great Falls. This was the era when semipro baseball dominated Paterson and was supported by passing the hat for donations during games.

The Smart Set were an all-Black team and asked him to play for them during summers, because at Eastside High his reputation had spread throughout North Jersey. Doby was a second baseman. Another former scholastic hero, Monte Irvin, from Orange High, was five years older than Larry and already on board at shortstop. Both of them moved on to the Newark Eagles of the Negro National League in 1942 and led them to a Black World Series championship in '46.

"He [Wilson] was a master of the fundamentals of the game," Doby said. "That's what he drilled into us, and that's the way we learned to play the game."

Later, when I interviewed Al Kachadurian, he was expansive about the times when he played not with Doby but against him and the Smart Set.

"He [Doby] was still growing, so the power had not been established yet," Al said. "He was more of a singles hitter. But if the ball was hit on the ground, his speed helped him beat it out. He always made contact. I was a catcher with the Chevy Red Sox. We were the two best semipro teams in Passaic County. We had a sponsor—I got twenty-five dollars a game—the Smart Set did not. But the people always turned out to see them. We had a great rivalry. Our team was all-white, they were all-Black, and every time we played the crowd packed Eastside Park or Hinchliffe. It was a great rivalry. Too bad that Doby is not here to tell you about those games—and John Ellerbee. Those guys could really play."

Ellerbee, primarily a third baseman, was more popular on the Paterson sandlots than either Irvin or Doby. When the Eagles signed Doby and Irvin away from Paterson, they wanted Ellerbee as well, but he declined.

Ellerbee later told WBGO's Doug Doyle, "I didn't want to go. I was married and had a kid. I didn't want to be on the road. I felt like the Smart Set was just as good as the Eagles. But we had a lot of fun when Monte and Larry played with me. I always hit around .375 or .385—I had the highest batting average of anyone I ever played with or against. I never even thought about the major leagues. We were Black . . . and they just were never gonna look at us, much less take us.

"So, no, I guess you could say I never made it, good as I was. But my cousin did. People would ask who he played for, and I would laugh and say, 'Everybody.' His name was Dizzy Gillespie. He played that horn day and night. He lived a few houses down the block, and he cost me a lot of sleep."

To play for the Smart Set became a real status symbol for a teenage kid. "Back then, I think I was the proudest when I would put on my Smart Set uniform," Doby told me. "People turned to look and wave when I walked through Paterson to the park for a game. People looked when they saw the uniform. I felt like I was part of something important in the community when I saw their reaction. At the time, those games drew the biggest crowds I played before."

"I do remember Mr. Wilson," Larry Jr. once told me. "He lived in Montclair, and after we moved there my dad used to take me with him when he visited. My dad wanted me to understand how much Mr. Wilson had meant to him."

All through high school, Larry Doby was a citywide hero. His church threw a banquet in his honor, with three hundred in attendance. His picture was a familiar sight on the sports pages of Paterson's two daily newspapers, the *Morning Call* and the *Evening News.* In a world where there was no chance for a Black man ever to play major-league baseball, Doby was nonetheless a genuine celebrity. With his classmates and the fans who packed Hinchliffe Stadium on autumn Saturdays to see him catch passes, and with the city's sports columnists, he was clearly a hometown hero. But the girl he had his eyes on never once saw him play a single inning of baseball. Her name was Helyn Curvy.

In his sophomore year, he had noticed her around the neighborhood as "that girl" when she walked past his house to school. He made it his mission to make her *his* girl.

At first, he waited in front of his home to walk her to school. Pretty soon, he was carrying her books. But Helyn still couldn't get to see him play a baseball game for Eastside. Her father had died, and her mother was working. While Doby was racking up record batting averages on the ball field, she was at home after school helping to raise three of her sisters. In response, Larry would take her brother, George, to watch him play and then bring him back home afterward so George could tell Helyn about the game.

It was not a pointless effort. As one of his teammates said, "Helyn Curvy was one beautiful girl. They dated all through high school. It was inevitable they would eventually marry."

"They were very much alike," Larry Doby Jr. said. "Growing up, I learned that if either one of them didn't want to do something, they wouldn't. That's why neither one of them would tell any of us about the bad times dad went through. They didn't want us to know. But I did learn one thing. It is also why they were totally committed to each other. I can remember the only time they had an argument out loud. It was over a bar he bought. She was totally against it, but I think she helped out when it opened.

"She was the one who got him through the darkest days. I know she used to tell him after a bad game or a racist incident at the ballpark, 'There's always tomorrow.' I don't think he ever made a serious decision without consulting her. And she could always make him laugh. In school he ran the 440, and there was a guy from Clifton, I think his name was Otto Stromeyer—dad could never beat him. Whenever she wanted to make him laugh, she would imitate a sports announcer: *And they are off in the 440. Doby breaks into the lead. He is finally going to . . . uh-oh—here comes Otto.*

"And then they would laugh."

If Doby were to make a living playing baseball after high school, it would have to be somewhere among the talent-rich,

Negro Leagues rosters. Most on his mind was the Newark Eagles, the legendary kings of all New Jersey Black baseball teams. The Eagles were owned by the most prominent husband-wife team in all of baseball, Abe and Effa Manley.

Most of the franchise owners in the Negro National League got their original incomes directly from the biggest street industry in their communities: the numbers racket. It was to blue-collar Blacks what the stock market was to white-collar investors. But this was not the numbers game of Dutch Schultz or Al Capone. The guys who ran the Black game always paid off. They were viewed as heroic entrepreneurs, figures who sponsored neighborhood sports teams and often sent indigent neighborhood kids to college. Some had their own soup kitchens during the Great Depression, but they also built fortunes off the dimes of the poorest of dreamers.

The Eagles were the result of a merger between the Brooklyn Eagles and the Newark Dodgers. Abe Manley was a baseball purist. He didn't want to negotiate salaries or league matters, or even manage the team. All he wanted to do was haunt the sandlots and find players. He gave all the other jobs to Effa. Ironically, she was the one inducted into the Baseball Hall of Fame, but it was Abe who found the players. Among them were seven eventually elected to the Hall of Fame.

Doby had no way of knowing it, but the Manleys would be his ticket to break white baseball's American League color line. What he also didn't know was that the Eagles were pressured from two different sources to sign him.

Monte Irvin, his old Smart Set teammate, explained his role in that to me like this: "We [the Eagles] had a first baseman named Len Pearson who was dating Helyn's sister. We went up to Paterson one day so that Pearson could see his girl. Eastside was playing baseball, so I went to see the game while Pearson was with her. I had forgotten the power in his swing. When I saw it again, I knew that high school was not the end. I knew this kid would be playing ball somewhere. When we got back home, I called Abe and told him he had to get up there and see this kid."

Irvin didn't know it, but a Black umpire who had worked a lot of Eastside games had already told Manley the same thing. Manley had never seen Doby play in person. In fact, he didn't know much about him. But he scheduled a tryout at Hinchliffe Stadium in Paterson, where the Eagles occasionally played and which had served as the home field for both the New York Black Yankees and the New York Cuban Giants. Abe was not disappointed.

As they watched, Effa asked, "What do you think?"

"He is good, and he'll get better. I want him."

Now it was in Effa's hands, and her job was to keep the payroll down. Later that night, Effa realized she was in the strangest negotiation she'd ever been part of, because money was barely discussed.

"I want your boy to come to Newark and play for us," Abe said to Etta. "We could pay him one hundred dollars a month," she added.

"That's nice," Etta replied. "But I have a few conditions. He is just eighteen years old, and you have a team of men. Like I said, I have a few conditions."

Lord, did Etta have conditions. Suddenly, everyone's role was reversed. Foremost among her demands were that he come directly home after games in Newark or sleep in the Manley house; that on the road he remain in his hotel room; that at all times the Manleys take personal responsibility for keeping him away from the evils of adult baseball players on long postgame evenings.

One element that she perceived as evil was the Grand Hotel on West Market Street in Newark. In a swinging city of jazz clubs, active nightlife, and a number of after-hours joints colloquially referred to as "blind pigs," Miss Etta worried most about the temptations of the Grand. The hotel was a lot of things, but evil was not one of them. It was there that the city's Black intelligentsia, professionals, musicians, celebrities, and, yes, the Eagles gathered nightly after home games. It was Etta's perception about the late-night intentions of the ballplayers that seemed to worry her.

In his terrific book *Effa Manley and the Newark Eagles*, James Overmyer indicated there were some genuine reasons a mother might have had that idea. As Overmyer wrote, "Women looking to make a connection with unattached ballplayers would sit on the side of the crowded ballroom and try to get the attention of players they had seen at Ruppert Stadium. If they didn't know his name, they would have him paged with his uniform number."

Abe promised that none of the above would impact her son. "I will see to that," he said.

"One more thing," Etta said just when it seemed the negotiations had ended. "There's basketball."

"What about it?" a weary Abe responded. "We don't play it."

"No," Etta said, "but he does, and he's very good. Coach Clair Bee over at LIU (a national basketball power) scouted him in high school and offered him a four-year scholarship. If he played for you, would he be able to keep the scholarship? I want him to go to college. Baseball is secondary."

"We can take care of that. Nobody will ever know. He'll be Larry Walker from Los Angeles. That's what the scorecard will say. We do that for kids all the time to protect their amateur standing." Money was not the issue—but Etta was able to raise Effa's offer from $100 a month to $300.

Etta was also looking for role models for young Larry. What she didn't realize was that the necessary role models for his future were right there with the Eagles—brilliant, mature athletes like Ray Dandridge, a bowlegged third baseman so skilled that when he played in Cuba a sportswriter wrote, "He was so bowlegged that you could pass a freight train between his legs but not a ground ball." There was a great right-handed pitcher named Leon Day, so talented that he never sat down—he played every game at some position and was a steady .350 hitter. There were others, too numerous to list here, and, of course, there was Monte Irvin, who became a lifelong friend.

"I was just eighteen and they were men," Doby told me. "Baseball was all they had. It wasn't a fraternity house. They did not exactly welcome another bat and a younger set of legs that could have taken their jobs." But what a faculty and what a group of baseball role models they were for the kid from Paterson.

The Eagles had yet to win a championship when Doby joined the team in 1942, but they were always in the hunt. The New York Yankees had built a world-class ballpark, Ruppert Stadium, for the Newark Bears, their Triple-A farm team. When the Bears went on the road, the Eagles moved in. Their Sunday games were a sight to behold. Those games were scheduled late in the afternoon to enable large church groups to leave for the stadium from church directly after services. Consequently, the Eagles drew the best-dressed fans in all of baseball. The men wore straw hats, the women wore their Sunday finest. It was every bit as much a social event as a ballgame.

The team Doby would join had a place in the very heartbeat of the city's Black community. Effa Manley was the single biggest reason. She was the lady whom local Black society's women would recruit to head their many community fundraisers. No white mayor of Newark would dare miss the Eagles' season opener—not if he wanted to be reelected. Among those who threw out ceremonial first pitches were Lena Horne and Joe Louis.

While the Eagles were good enough to compete, Abe knew they were nowhere near strong enough to catch the Homestead Grays, who'd won eight titles in nine years. But the team he was building back then was talented and exciting and was headed in the right direction. Knowledgeable Eagles fans understood that—their loyalty was unshakable on every level of the city, from the Black movers and shakers right on down to the ladies of a prominent bordello, who never missed a home game.

As a case in point, the Eagles were rarely booed. But first baseman Fran Matthews told Overmyer of a time he made a crucial error and was roundly booed. Heading for the bench, he heard surprising encouragement from several ladies seated behind his dugout. Not surprising, given that it was ladies' day. What he heard was "Don't worry, baby. We are all with you." He recognized the cheerleaders as the madam of a local brothel and some of her girls.

Everybody loved the Eagles. They were Black baseball's original schedule-it-and-they-will-come home team. On Sundays and holidays, they drew crowds of 13,000 or more when they played at Ruppert Stadium. Visiting teams loved playing in

Newark, just a twelve-minute train ride from the bright lights of Manhattan, and Newark itself offered a vibrant Black nightlife.

Some of the league's less-affluent franchises were quick to take notice. One year, the Baltimore Elite Giants moved all their scheduled home games with the Eagles to Newark. Part of that lure was the Eagles' "underground advertising network": Posters for important upcoming Eagles home games magically appeared in every Black grocery store, shoeshine parlor, and barbershop. Just as white fans debated the talents of Joe DiMaggio and Mel Ott, the Black barbershops echoed with arguments over which pitcher was more valuable to his team: Satchel Paige or the Eagles' Leon Day.

The only major disappointment among the devoted Eagles fans was that the Yankees-owned Newark Bears of the International League, who shared their stadium with the Eagles, repeatedly turned down Abe Manley's offer to play an exhibition series for charity against the Bears. "At the time," Irvin told me, "the players wanted that game more than Abe did."

The Eagles with Doby and Irvin would finally bring Effa and Abe their only Black World Series championship in 1946, when they defeated the Kansas City Monarchs of the Black American League in seven games. That season Doby hit .365, led the league in hits and triples, and made the All-Star team. He had no idea or warning, but the following summer he would be the one Bill Veeck chose to break the American League color line with the Cleveland Indians.

CHAPTER 5

THE RISE AND FALL OF THE MANLEYS, AND THE EAGLES' LAST FLIGHT

Larry Walker (née Doby) from Los Angeles reported to the Newark Eagles without advance excitement in LA, probably because Doby had never been west of West Orange, New Jersey. Moreover, since Paterson was home to two Negro League teams, its Black population paid no attention to the Eagles, because there was virtually nowhere for the fans to read about them.

The only Eagle who recognized Doby was Monte Irvin, who'd played with him for the semipro Smart Set. Abe Manley, the man who signed him, had a habit of forgetting to tell managers whom he had signed. As a case in point, Monte once told me that when he reported to Willie Wells, the team's player-manager, he asked Irvin who the hell he was. Irvin replied he was the new shortstop.

"I don't think so," said Wells, one of the greatest shortstops in Negro League baseball. "Far as I know, we only got one shortstop: me. See all that green out there? That's the outfield. Go find a position there."

Not only did Wells consider Irvin a stranger, but he also set in motion the only position Irvin would play when he integrated the New York Giants of the majors' National League. The only thing Wells knew about Doby was that he would be the youngest member of the Eagles, and since he was Larry Walker now, his Eastside reputation would not precede him.

Newark was vastly different back then. The huge concrete coffins that served as public housing had yet to be built. As Connie Woodruff, a featured Black reporter at several newspapers and an expert on the city's social life and mores, told Overmyer for his book on Effa Manley, "Newark had always been a big small town, more metropolitan now than when I was growing up."

Without the towering public housing, families migrating from the South in search of better jobs lived in shared housing with their extended families until they were established and able to move out on their own. That meant the "front stoop" was where, on hot summer nights, they gathered and shared their thoughts of the neighborhood.

Woodruff also shared with Overmyer an undeniable truth. From stoop to stoop, church to church, and barbershop to barbershop, the Eagles were a major part of those conversations.

This was only natural. Newark, the state's largest city, was forever in the shadow of New York. Just as its white baseball fans viewed the record-setting Newark Bears as their civic answer to New York's three major-league teams, so it was in the Black community with the Eagles. Larry Doby joined the Eagles with his LIU basketball scholarship "legally" protected by his false identity, just as Etta Doby had demanded.

He was asked throughout his life about the first time he played against the powerful Homestead Grays. His favorite story involved catcher Josh Gibson: "My first time up, Josh said, 'We're going to find out if you can hit a fastball.' I singled. Next time up, Josh said, 'We're going to find out if you can hit a curveball.' I singled. Third time up, Josh said, 'We're going to find out how you do after you're knocked down.' I popped up the first time after they knocked me down. The second time, I singled."

As Larry Walker from Los Angeles or Larry Doby from Paterson, after he'd been once around the league it was clear this was no ordinary rookie. Effa Manley sensed he was a product to be promoted. Hence, articles started to find their way into the Black press:

Chicago Defender—"Although playing his first year as a professional baseball player, Larry Walker looks good as most veterans. He hits well and is a dependable infielder."

Baltimore Afro-American—"Larry Walker of Los Angeles made his Negro National League debut last Sunday with the Newark Eagles, singled and later scored on a hit by Leon Day as the Eagles beat the New York Cubans, 8–3, before 17,000 at Yankee Stadium."

New York Age—"Larry Walker, the new Eagles center fielder . . . has become an overnight sensation. He plays his position like a veteran and his hitting is part of the team's strength."

All those accolades and more, but only one of his Eagles teammates, Monte Irvin, even knew that Larry Doby was still a month away from his high school graduation. He broke into the lineup at third base, was moved to second, then to first, switched to the outfield, and by season's end was back at second base. Either he was the most versatile rookie in the league or his manager couldn't figure out where to put him. But one thing was clear: with a bat like his, he had to be somewhere in the lineup. When he first reported, his age made his teammates view him as a kind of mascot. But once they saw him hit, there was no doubt this rookie could play ball.

Still, his soft-spoken demeaner and reclusive adherence to his mother's rules ("Stay in your hotel room on the road") combined to make Walker (née Doby) somewhat isolated from his teammates and their nocturnal celebrations. Not that there was much to celebrate in 1942. The Eagles finished third. A year later they were fourth, a disappointing 22 1/2 games behind the Homestead Grays.

But none of this dampened enthusiasm among locals.

For starters, nobody was going to beat the Grays, unless it was the Monarchs, if they got to the Negro League World Series. By the mid-1940s, that was almost axiomatic. But Abe and Effa were quietly putting the necessary pieces in place.

World War II was about to decimate the Eagles, but when the boys came marching home in 1946, the Manleys would emerge as the new sheriffs in town. Wearing the two brightest stars would be the old Smart Set twins, Irvin and Doby. Together, they would eventually help bring all the long-suffering Eagles fans their first and only World Series title.

And, ironically, the individual excellence of both would eventually play key roles in the integration of Major League Baseball, which put the Manleys out of business. But until that day, the loyalty of the Eagles' fan base was unwavering despite their futile pursuit of the Grays, the Pittsburgh Crawfords, and, occasionally, even the Baltimore Elite Giants. One of the things that kept Eagles fans unified and faithful was the work of Sherman "Jocko" Maxwell, a post office worker in Newark. He loved what he saw in young Doby, loved the Eagles, and, most of all, loved baseball.

Just as the game was horrendously segregated, so was Maxwell's uphill effort to be the first Black man to broadcast it.

Jocko Maxwell was sixteen years older than Larry Doby. Years before Doby fought what I consider the loneliest battle in the game's history—even lonelier than Jackie Robinson's—Jocko had been there, done that, and won.

In the days before computers, newspapers archived crucial articles by cutting them out and filing them. That department was known as the morgue. At the *Star-Ledger* it was run by Jocko's father, William, and his family. He was an honors graduate from Dunbar High School, in Washington, DC. Racially segregated, it still offered classic curricula. William ran our morgue for years with his oldest son, Emerson. His daughter was our front desk receptionist, and Jocko was just there constantly.

A postal worker by day and the only Black radio sportscaster in America by night, Jocko once deliberately failed a final exam at Newark's Central High School, delaying his graduation, in order for him to play another baseball season. He managed a semipro team called the Newark Starlings. He haunted Black radio stations in Newark and New York and became an unpaid on-air sportscaster, eventually getting a salary from several stations to the point where his reputation went national. He knew Effa and Abe Manley, and became the public-address announcer for their games at Ruppert Stadium.

Eagles fans got their print news from the *Afro-American* and other Black metropolitan newspapers and, of course, from Jocko, who also performed one other serious service. Because of his family connection, he induced the *Star-Ledger* to run Eagles line scores, then box scores, and finally articles—all compiled by himself for no salary. He did it by reminding the sports editor that both Doby and Irvin had been *Star-Ledger* all-staters as high schoolers. As a result, the local Black community was probably the only such group in the country that could read about its team consistently in a white-owned newspaper.

The hardcore loyalty of the Eagles' fan base was well established. Abe Manley had replaced some aging key players with new signees and shrewdly traded for others. He even had a chance to sign the biggest box-office attraction in both Black baseball leagues.

Satchel Paige was still jumping between teams. At that point he was pitching for the Pittsburgh Crawfords and feuding with their owner, Gus Greenlee, who called Effa Manley and said, "You can have the son of a bitch cheap. I'm tired of him."

It did not take long before she got a letter from Satchel: "I agree to join the Eagles if you will become my sideline girlfriend." History doesn't tell us for sure who wrote the reply—Abe or Effa. It simply read, "Stay where you are."

Still, the Eagles were on the verge of making a run, or so Abe and Effa thought. Unfortunately, Germany and Japan refused to cooperate. The war came between Larry Doby and the championship of all the Black baseball world. On July 23, 1943, Doby, who had been drafted into the Navy, left for active duty.

All of a sudden, just when Effa and Abe thought they could finally claim a title, key pieces were otherwise occupied. Max Manning was feverishly driving a gasoline truck, trying to keep up with General Patton's speeding armored troops. Monte Irvin was constructing bridges under heavy fire. Doby, who had been assigned as a physical training instructor at Great Lakes, was on his way to a Pacific atoll halfway between the Caroline Islands and the Philippines to participate in the pending massive invasion of Japan meant to end the war. In all, the Manleys lost seven key players to the military. At war's end, they all returned.

What choice did they have? As Doby once told me, "It figured. We were never as happy as the days we rode their bus. We sang, we laughed, we needled each other. We didn't even think about the white leagues. It was clear they were never going to want us. So we didn't waste time worrying about that. We were getting paid to play a great game we all loved. When the season ended, we followed the sun to Puerto Rico, Mexico, Cuba, and Venezuela. No prejudice, no segregation. We ate where we wanted, we slept where we wanted, and sometimes our families came with us."

It was a life of attitudes. Segregated as they were in America, those team-bus riders had something nobody could change, steal, or take away. The bases were always ninety feet apart; three strikes or four balls; nine innings unless God decided to rain on you; and hell, which was an act of God, not of the Klan.

I am reminded of a time long after Doby broke the American League color line . . . long after the Eagles were dead, as was the Negro National League. It was a time when the great Eagles pitcher Leon Day was dying in a Baltimore hospital and his old teammate Max Manning had come to say goodbye.

During that emotional hour, Day had voiced exactly what every Negro League player believed about the dignity Black baseball gave them. It was the day the Veterans Committee was meeting to see if they would vote Leon into the Baseball Hall of Fame. A nurse came into the room accompanied by a white reporter. In her hand she held a baseball.

"Mr. Day," she said, "this man is from the *Baltimore Sun*, and he has something to tell you."

"Mr. Day," said the reporter, "it is my honor to let you know that you have just been voted into the Baseball Hall of Fame."

Leon looked at Max and winked. "That's nice."

The nurse handed Leon the ball and asked him to sign it. Weak as he was, he gripped the ball firmly and wrote, "Leon Day. H.O.F." Then he fell back against his pillow.

"Mr. Day, no offense, and I hope you will understand why I must ask this," the reporter said. "Does this take away any of the disappointment of being kept out of the big leagues?"

Leon looked at Max and winked again. "Young man, you have been seriously misinformed. I played in the big leagues all my life. But I don't know if some of the white boys you are thinking of could have played in mine." And both Leon and Max believed every word of that.

So, yes, the military Eagles were coming home just as soon as the ink on their honorable discharges could dry. They had unfinished business.

Patience was all that Manley had left: patience to wait for their "boys" to come marching home . . . patience to wait for the chance to win a pennant . . . patience before they could put the Homestead Grays and Gus Greenlee in their place. Both of the latter two goals were formidable. The Grays had won two straight Negro World Series titles. But Effa was supremely confident, as always, that it would happen and that she and Abe would emerge holding the winning cards. So she did what Effa always did.

Negro Leagues Baseball Museum

Larry Doby as a Newark Eagle.

Negro Leagues Baseball Museum

Abe and Effa Manley, owners of the Newark Eagles, who sent Doby to the Cleveland Indians.

Getty Images

Jackie Robinson and Larry Doby photographed together for the first time.

Getty Images

Doby and Steve Gromek in the photo seen 'round the world.

Getty Images

Indians skipper Lou Boudreau (left), along with Doby (center) and general manager Hank Greenberg (right).

Getty Images

Doby and Satchel Paige—the first two African Americans in the American League—with coach Bill McKechnie.

Getty Images

The first Black All-Stars (left to right): Roy Campanella, Doby, Don Newcombe, and Robinson.

Getty Images

Welcome Home, Larry! The city of Paterson, New Jersey, welcomes Doby with a parade in his honor.

Getty Images

(left to right) Suitcase Simpson, Willie Mays, and Doby in Atlanta to receive the "Inspiration for Youth" award.

Getty Images

After a decade in Cleveland, Doby was traded to the Chicago White Sox in 1956.

The Star Ledger, Newark, New Jersey

At last! Commissioner Bud Selig presents Larry Doby with his Hall of Fame plaque, almost forty years after his last game.

The Star Ledger, Newark, New Jersey

The Star Ledger, Newark, New Jersey

Helyn Doby with pure joy as Hall of Famer Don Newcombe shares the special moment.

The Star Ledger, Newark, New Jersey

Doby wiping away tears after his emotional Hall of Fame speech.

Courtesy of the author

Larry Doby presents author Jerry Izenberg with his National Sportscasters and Sportswriters Association Hall of Fame plaque.

The Star Ledger, Newark, New Jersey

Speaking to the students of Jersey City State College after accepting an honorary doctorate from the university.

The Star Ledger, Newark, New Jersey

(left to right) Yogi Berra, Doby, and Phil Rizzuto at New Jersey's first Hall of Fame Night.

The Star Ledger, Newark, New Jersey

Doby sits with his grandson and daughter at a ceremony naming baseball fields at Paterson's Eastside Park in his honor.

Getty Images

On the 50th anniversary of breaking the American League color line, Doby speaks to the fans in Cleveland on July 5, 1997.

Getty Images

With his number retired by the Indians in 1994, Doby's No. 14 is displayed prominently outside Progressive Park.

The Star Ledger, Newark, New Jersey

The Star Ledger, Newark, New Jersey

Lifelong friends Joe Taub and Larry Doby tour the old neighborhood and share a laugh.

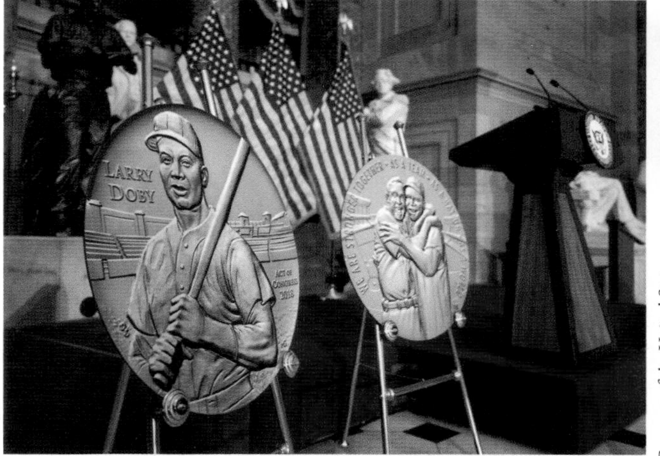

Congress of the United States

Front and back of medal, with the back image being the famous hug between Doby and Steve Gromek.

Congress of the United States

Larry Doby Jr. and New Jersey's Honorable Bill Pascrell Jr., US House of Representatives.

Getty Images

They never forgot. Statue of Doby guards the entrance of Progressive Field.

She adapted. She ran benefits and sales of war bonds. She took busloads of Black entertainers and musicians to perform for Black soldiers at Fort Dix. She went to parties, often without Abe.

Connie Woodruff's interview with Overmyer explained a lot of things about that: "Effa shifted back and forth between high society and the 'others,' Woodruff said. "She wasn't overly friendly to women. Effa could have passed for White, and she may have been overly friendly to males, don't make a mistake about that. The Black community had a caste system [based on light versus dark complexion]. Her husband was very dark. He was much older. When you are young, that matters a lot."

But in their profession—Abe the talent scout and Effa the no-nonsense businesswoman—they were a perfect team. She never doubted that they would ultimately put the Grays and their owner, Gus Greenlee, in their place.

When Doby arrived in 1945 on Ulithi, a volcanic atoll in the Caroline Islands, he had never heard of it, much less understood its significance in what could have been both the finale and the war's bloodiest battle. He learned that the steady seaborne traffic around the island was the direct result of marking it as a major staging area for the Navy during its final push to secure the Philippines and begin the invasion of Japan. The place could have been the flashpoint of the battle to end the biggest geographical war in our history. Larry Doby, from Paterson, New Jersey, was suddenly stationed on what could have been the fuse.

Each morning he looked at the sea from one of the largest coral reef lagoons in the world and saw as many as seven hundred ships. The 323rd Regiment combat team of the 81st Infantry had captured the island without a fight. Then the Seabees came and built everything the fleet needed. They built another airstrip on Mogmog Island, which also became home to R&R facilities, including sports fields.

Mogmog was where Doby met another ballplayer. For years, Mickey Vernon had been an All-Star and the best hitter on the Washington Senators. In off-duty hours, the white major-leaguer and the Black Negro Leaguer ran two pick-up teams; watching Doby's classic swing, Vernon knew he was looking at a guy who belonged in the big leagues.

It was while they were there that they heard, on Armed Forces Radio, the news that Jackie Robinson had signed to play for the Brooklyn Dodgers' Montreal farm club.

"This could be your chance," Vernon told Doby. And that was how the famous letter to Clark Griffith, touting Doby's skills, was written by the best player Griffith had—and how rudely the man who owned the Senators rejected it.

Doby never forgot Vernon's gesture.

When Doby returned to the Eagles, Vernon shipped him an armful of bats. Doby never forgot that either.

In August 1945, it became clear that an assault on the Japanese mainland was unnecessary. The use of the atomic bomb ended the war. Larry and all the other Eagles returned to Newark and helped Effa and Abe Manley finally realize their dream deferred.

The season began on May 5, 1946, with an omen straight out of a B-movie. It was Opening Day at Ruppert Stadium. Red, white, and blue bunting adorned the grandstand walls in a perfect semicircle. Effa, in a new dress, wore an aurora borealis of a smile. Abe was busily counting the house while Leon Day was completing his warmups.

For nine straight innings, Day mowed down the Philadelphia Stars. They couldn't muster up anything approximating a hit. Effa and Abe must have looked up at game's end, savored the row of zeroes that signified Day's no-hitter, and seen their ultimate goal just beyond the horizon. The league format divided the season in half, the winner of each half to meet in a playoff. But the Eagles destroyed every roadblock.

They won the first half; they won the second half. Best of all, they clinched the first half by beating the Grays three out of four. Irvin hit .369, Doby .365. But Larry slammed 85 hits, five more than Monte. The Eagles had a record home attendance of more than 120,000.

In addition to Doby's emergence as a key building block in the team's near future, he chose the championship season to solve a problem he had not realized he'd been running away from since his return from Mogmog. He had begun to date Helyn Curvy again. Now he was seeing more and more of her.

In midseason, Helyn changed the rules. She told him it was time to marry her or time to forget the whole thing. They were married in Paterson on August 10. The Eagles had a game in Trenton that night.

After they left the church, they were caught in a midsummer downpour. Somebody up there must have liked them because the game was canceled, and were able to celebrate their wedding night without distraction.

By September, half the record flight of the Eagles' mission was accomplished. Now came the toughest part. Ahead lay the Negro

League World Series and the Kansas City Monarchs, with Leroy "Satchel" Paige, the legend whom Effa Manley had once rejected.

Together they played what must have been the greatest of all Negro League World Series. Its sheer drama lasted right up until the final out of the seventh game. Since both teams had won both halves of their season, no playoffs were necessary. That gave them ample time to promote their "dream matchup."

It resulted in the most interest that the Negro League World Series had ever generated. The league offices agreed: if people from New York and Chicago couldn't get to the Series, they would take the Series to them.

Game One would be played in Harlem at the Polo Grounds, home of the New York Giants of the National League, and Game Five would be in Comiskey Park, home of the American League White Sox. Harlem was the home of Sugar Hill, where Black celebrities, musicians, and intellectuals lived. Comiskey, close to the heavily Black section known as Bronzeville, once drew 51,723, for the league's 1943 All-Star game.

Each D train on New York's subway line was packed that morning as it rumbled through the underground darkness on Tuesday until it stopped on the platform at 155th Street. The riders exited, turned right, and climbed a set of narrow stairs reaching toward the light. At ground level, the outer walls of the Polo Grounds loomed before them.

The fans of the Newark Eagles flowed to the entrance gates. They were headed toward Effa and Abe's dream machine, the first step on the highway toward a Black baseball fan's Promised Land.

Newark's National League team of never-won-it/never-even-been-there versus the swagger of Satchel Paige and his well-established Kansas City Monarchs . . . a dream matchup between two franchises featuring a handful of future defectors, whose successful integration would eventually doom both leagues. Paige was the difference in Game One—both as a relief pitcher and as a hitter who singled and scored the winning run in a 2–1 victory.

The series then moved on to Ruppert Stadium in Newark. With the advantage of playing close to home, Doby's home run helped bring the Eagles back in a six-run seventh-inning rally that battered Paige in his second relief stint. The Eagles' 7–4 win tied the series at one game each. But with the next two games at Blues Stadium in Kansas City, the Monarchs won the next one with humiliating ease, 15–5. Still, the Eagles fought back and tied the series at two games apiece with an 8–1 victory behind Rufus Lewis's four-hitter.

For Game Five, the teams moved to the big-league stadium that the Monarchs had chosen: Comiskey Park on Chicago's South Side. With its large Black population, Satch and the Monarchs were no strangers there. But the game drew the smallest crowd of the series—around 4,000—and the Eagles played like they had given up. They left six men on base in the first three innings and never managed a serious threat, losing 5–1.

That put Newark on life support. Lose Game Six and the dream was dead. Clinging to life by a metaphorical eyelash and with the final two games at Ruppert Stadium, the Eagles battled back. It was Irvin who became the hero with a solo home run in the sixth that held up for a 9–7 equalizer and set up Game Seven.

So this was what Abe Manley had envisioned when he sat in Etta Doby's kitchen and listened to what she expected him to do for her son. This was what he expected when he took Monte Irvin away from the Smart Set's pass-the-hat sandlot games. This was what he discovered when he was introduced to Effa at a

World Series game, and was fascinated by her business acumen almost as much as her beauty. This was where the dream came together and took him from the high rental price and the empty seats at Ebbets Field in Brooklyn to Newark, accompanied by the two most important things in his life: Effa and his ballclub.

It took him to this day, September 29, 1946, with about 10,000 fans in the seats and his team in brand-new white uniforms that Effa insisted the occasion warranted. It was a game that Abe, Effa, and the city had spent eleven years waiting for. What they got was a nail-biting pitchers' duel. The Eagles jumped to a 1–0 lead in the first on Irvin's RBI single. The Monarchs stranded five baserunners in the first five innings. Meanwhile, the pitchers were putting on a clinic. Then Buck O'Neil hit one out in the sixth and it was tied, 1–1.

But in the bottom of the inning, Doby and Irvin drew walks and Johnnie Davis doubled to left, scoring both runners. Nobody relaxed. Rufus Lewis for the home team and the Monarchs' Ford Smith were near perfect. Lewis would hold the visitors to eight scattered hits and Ford was even better, limiting the Eagles to just three.

Trailing 2–1 in the bottom of the eighth, the Monarchs did not go quietly into failure. Incredibly, two singles and a walk with one out produced nothing because the second runner was thrown out trying to stretch his hit into a double. Two down in the ninth, the batter was Herb Souell. Lewis came in high and tight. Souell swung. And as first baseman Lennie Pearson circled under the harmless popup, a great wail of a cry rocked the ballpark. Pearson squeezed it—and the party began.

And of course it spilled over into the Grand Hotel later that night.

In his autobiography, the late author Amiri Baraka explained what it meant to the very core of Newark's Black community. It was more than a ballgame:

"The Eagles were legitimate Black Heroes . . . pure love . . . in the laughter and noise and colors and easy hot dogs, there was something of us celebrating ourselves. . . . In the flying around the bases and sliding and home runs, arguments, and triumphs there was more of ourselves in celebration than we were normally ever permitted. It was ours."

Read that carefully and you will understand what Larry Doby and Monte Irvin and those born too soon to follow their footsteps meant to those who played before.

Abe and Effa had reached the top of the mountain they had worked so hard to climb. But after the euphoria, little did they know that there was no place to go but down.

CHAPTER 6

WHITE SCOUTS ON THE HUNT, EFFA ON THE PHONE, A TOILET KIT, AND FIFTY DOLLARS

Bill Veeck's head tried to tell him what he really wanted, but even before he listened, his instincts were preparing the way. Son of Chicago sportswriter William Veeck Sr., Veeck grew up in the suburb of Hinsdale, Illinois. When Bill was four, his father became president of the Chicago Cubs. By the time Bill was eleven, he was working as a vendor, ticket seller, and junior groundskeeper. It was Bill Jr. who physically planted the iconic ivy on the outfield wall at Wrigley Field. He even worked across town in the business office of the White Sox.

Genetically, he seemed programmed for the next step. In 1940, he bought the independent Triple-A Milwaukee Brewers, and he sold the franchise five years later for a $275,000 profit. For part of that time, he was in the Marine Corps and lost his right leg in 1943 because of the recoil of an artillery piece during combat at Bougainville in the South Pacific. For much of his life he was a cigarette chain smoker, and as part of his unique personality he drilled holes in his wooden leg, often detached it, and used it as an ashtray while being interviewed. To add to the legend, as an owner-fan he rarely wore a suit or a sports jacket to a game. The writers nicknamed him "Sport Shirt Bill."

Veeck could generally be found walking through the cheap seats and shaking hands with fans, illustrating an old theory of his that it was there that the fans with the highest baseball IQs were to be located. "I find," he said, "baseball knowledge is highest there and lowest in the more expensive seats." When he owned his minor-league Brewers, he would sit up there during spring training in racially segregated Florida. It was also where, by law, Black fans sat.

When the sheriff pointed that out, he demanded Veeck move out of the section.

Veeck replied, "I own this team. If you want me to move, I will move, all right—straight out of Florida, and take my team with me. I am not getting out of this seat. Send for the mayor. You can explain that to him—if you dare." After the mayor was apprised, Veeck won by technical knockout in the first round and stayed right where he was every day of spring training.

Back in his youth, Veeck learned that the skin color of the pitcher meant nothing. What counted was how well he threw the ball. He figured that out when he attended home games of the all-Black Chicago American Giants and the traditional annual Negro Leagues All-Star game at Comiskey Park. He was the high bidder when the Philadelphia Phillies went up for sale, and planned to sign the best Negro League players to shatter the color line. When that got back to the commissioner's office, the bid was declined in order to keep baseball lily-white.

Finally, 1946 was the year he let his head listen to both his instincts and his heart. He had purchased the Cleveland Indians, and a reporter for the *Pittsburgh Courier*, an influential Black newspaper, asked him about the color line. He casually replied, "I fully expect one day when the Indians take the field, there will be a colored player among them."

A year later, with no fanfare, he called Indians scout Bill Killefer into his office, pledged him to secrecy, and assigned him to track both Negro Leagues with emphasis on the progress of the Eagles' Larry Doby. Veeck also hired a Black promoter and PR man named Lou Jones to scrutinize the off-the-field demeanor of the men Killefer thought were his most likely candidates.

Jones was a former Pittsburgh political figure and the ex-husband of singer-actress Lena Horne. In their dating days they were often seen in the Pittsburgh clubs favored by prestigious Black couples. Nightlife and fast times were no mystery to Jones. If something was going on in Doby's private life, he would find it.

Somehow Veeck gained access to the thoughts of Dodgers scout Clyde Sukeforth, the man who signed Jackie Robinson and was still scouting both Negro Leagues. Sukeforth was a regular at Eagles home games.

From Killefer, he learned that Doby was a major-league hitter. After all the games he watched and on which he kept meticulous notes, Killefer came to what would be a prophetic conclusion. "I don't have the slightest clue where you can play him, but with his bat you will have to play him somewhere." Jones learned that Doby didn't "drink, smoke, gamble, or carouse." Sukeforth thought Doby was "a good player who would probably need one or two years' seasoning in the minors."

Meanwhile, Doby, who never even had a hint about any of this, was indeed proving he had a bat that demanded a spot in any lineup. He didn't know Killefer or Jones and had no way of knowing that after thirty games of the Eagles' 1947 season, he would be on his way to making history.

He had spent the offseason settling down with his new bride, Helyn, in the same Carroll Street neighborhood where he lived when he had first arrived in Paterson as a teenager. Now, as an All-Star member of the defending World Series champions, Doby was in nobody's shadow. Over those 30 games he hit .354. He believed he would be an Eagle forever.

But Effa Manley had her own ideas. The Black World Series title gave Abe a misleading sense of security. Effa, as always, took a long, hard look at what lay ahead. Jackie Robinson's arrival was an indisputable fact. That Black baseball fans started saving their disposable income so they could travel as far as Baltimore to see Jackie play was likewise indisputable. And their chance to actually see him in a Dodgers game meant that the Eagles had started to lose their after-church-Sunday-picnic fans. The sharp decline of her team's ticket sales was an omen she could not ignore. The title she and Abe fought so hard to secure was revealed as an empty promise of fool's gold as the Eagles' attendance began to drop. She began to see the future, and she began to think that she wouldn't be in it.

One suspects that for her the shift of Black baseball loyalty to support Jackie Robinson was a road map delineating disaster for both Negro Leagues. With that on her mind, she was quoted as saying that Larry Doby was the best prospect in baseball. "He can do everything Jackie Robinson can." It was a warning to anybody who wanted Larry that they damn well better be prepared to negotiate with her or get prepared for her lawsuit.

She and Abe knew they were coming to decision time. Abe, the gambler he'd always been since his days in the numbers game in Jersey City, held out for a trial year to see if it could all be turned around. Effa, who respected his love of the game, gave him two years. Either way they pretty much agreed that much sooner than later the Eagles would be dead.

The main reason for such preparation was due to when Branch Rickey came calling, who had virtually stolen her star pitcher Don Newcombe for the Dodgers without paying her a penny, or even talking to her about it. He had done the same with the Monarchs in Robinson's case, and with Roy Campanella. Rickey had also secretly signed Monte Irvin for a separate Negro League he was allegedly planning, perhaps as a cover story for bringing Robinson to the Dodgers. Effa took it as a personal insult the eventual use of Irvin's contract to steal a second player from the Eagles without her permission. She was enraged and, with a sharper eye than most baseball writers, took revenge in posing a relevant question: "Yes, he had Ebbets Field, but who else would rent a ballpark to him?" Defeated but not embarrassed, Rickey reluctantly backed down and cut Irvin loose when she publicly challenged his ethics.

Rickey, who was never afflicted with an attack of modesty, had always characterized his role in baseball as the man who fought for integration. In his book *Invisible Men*, Don Rogosin accurately quotes Rickey saying after he signed Robinson, "I couldn't face my God any longer knowing that his Black children were held separate and distinct from his white children in a game that has given me all I own."

But it was Wendell Smith, the great columnist with the *Pittsburgh Courier*, who earlier had written that before Brooklyn Rickey had been totally in charge of the St. Louis Cardinals and refused to rent Sportsman's Park to the all-Black St. Louis Stars when the Cardinals were on the road. "He said, 'St. Louis could support only one team,'" according to Smith.

For the record, the Cardinals actually had a Jim Crow seating section for their own home games. "That form of segregation was enforced by management [Rickey]. It was a blot on Rickey's record," Smith wrote.

Coincidentally, it is worth noting that before Veeck negotiated with the Manleys for Doby, he asked Smith for an opinion about Doby and was told, "He can play, and I've seen him enough to know. When it comes to talent, he is ready."

Nobody mentioned much about Rickey and the St. Louis Cardinals' Jim Crow sections once Robinson was signed, but after Rickey's failed attempt to "steal" Irvin's contract, he reached out and tried to turn the Black media against the Manleys as obstructionists standing in the way of Black players in search of serious opportunity. The backlash was intense.

Then came Veeck, convinced by Killefer and Jones that Doby could do it, angered by Rickey and with an eye on the Eagles' falling attendance. Effa met with Veeck. She and Abe needed money, and Veeck needed Doby. It was an inevitable marriage. The deal was done for $10,000 after thirty days. Veeck did this because Effa, knowing his dedication to civil rights, lectured him on the way other Black owners had been treated by Major League Baseball. After Effa agreed to Veeck's offer, she said to him, "If Larry Doby were white and a free agent, you'd give him $100,000 to sign as a bonus." The reason Effa pressured him for more money was that she knew he was a good man and she relied on that in their negotiations.

Veeck's devotion to the struggle for civil rights was no illusion. Twenty years later, in 1967, after Veeck had founded a fair-housing committee, the activist Rap Brown instigated a riot over housing in Cambridge, Maryland. The peace that ended it was negotiated on Veeck's front porch between demonstrators and the commander of the Maryland National Guard.

"I can remember that like it was yesterday," Mike Veeck recalled. "Three of them on our front porch: Dick Gregory, the activist-comedian; the general who commanded the Maryland National Guard; and my dad. Coincidentally, because the downtown movie theater was segregated, Dad showed films in our barn and opened them to everyone."

During her negotiations with Veeck, Effa offered a bonus of her own. "I have another player named Monte Irvin who might really be of help to you. He's good. Right now, he and Doby are fighting for the batting title. I'll let you have him for another thousand." Veeck said he told her he didn't know whether Cleveland was ready for two Black players. The Yankees should have thanked him for walking away at that point—with both Doby and Irvin in their lineup, the Indians might have replaced them as "America's Team."

Irvin later wound up with the New York Giants. That deal presented a dynamic anecdote about Effa's negotiating style. She had talked Veeck into the $5,000 bonus if Doby made it through thirty days. She did it by switching herself into the role of her victimization by Rickey and appealing to Veeck's conscience.

Rickey called Horace Stoneham of the Giants, knowing how much he had declined to pay her for Irvin. Rickey told Stoneham, "Get Doby. I think she will sell him for $5,000. Think what Irvin against Robinson can do for both of our box offices."

Stoneham took the bait and came away with a skillful player. This is the story Irvin told me: "I asked her for half the purchase price, because I had been loyal. She said, 'I have this guy in Newark who did all our legal work and never got paid. Don't you think he deserves half?'

"I told her yes, but you still have the other half.

"'Now, about the other half. I walked past Chesloff Furs on Halsey Street the other day and saw this fur jacket in the window for $2,500. Monte, I never had a fur jacket. I always wanted one. What do you think I should do?'

"She knew Monte far too well for his own good.

"Buy it, Mrs. Manley," he said, as she'd expected. "You deserve it."

In all those years negotiating with the tough other Negro League owners, some of whom had serious mob connections, Effa Manley had succeeded by alternatingly using her femininity and what she portrayed as her victimization. One of her tools was to cry at will to touch their consciences and, with a disarming smile, to utilize her propensity for hardball salary negotiations with her own players. Nobody was ever shrewd enough to beat her except Branch Rickey, who often publicly and without shame used phony pseudo-religious arguments to portray her as an obstacle to the advancement of her own race.

But Veeck wasn't Rickey. He believed Black players belonged in Major League Baseball. More to the point, he believed in Doby and knew Effa had no bargaining chips—but he also genuinely believed in fairness and civil rights. He opened a building to show films because the local theater was segregated, and he worked for fair housing.

So why did Veeck ignore the advice of some of his people who wanted Doby to be assigned to the minors first? The Dodgers sent Robinson to Montreal for a year—a city with no legal segregation and no great racist animus. But the Indians had only one Double-A farm team (Oklahoma City) and one Triple-A team (Baltimore) suitable for a player of Doby's experience—both were legally segregated cities, and both, through years of cultural indoctrination, were loaded with racial animus. Cleveland was tough, Veeck reasoned, but not as tough as the minors would have been for Doby in cities like Oklahoma City and Baltimore.

As preparation, Veeck had Jones meet well in advance of Doby's major-league debut with the crème de la crème of Cleveland's white industrial and business community leaders to set the stage. History shows Veeck probably should have met with the twenty Indians who refused to shake Doby's hand when he reported. Historically, this was one problem Jackie Robinson did not have in his own locker room. To his credit, Rickey would never tolerate it. Conversely, Indians manager Lou Boudreau, for whatever reason, never spoke out.

Doby did not know Robinson in the beginning. Robinson played in Kansas City for a short time, and the KC team was in the other Negro League. But that summer the two often spoke on the telephone. They compared their mutual problems and discussed mutual solutions, most of which did not exist.

But it was Doby's relief, in reflection years later, when he said to me, "In one way I think I was better off than Jackie. By breaking in at Montreal and Brooklyn, he had to go through the crap twice during road trips. I went directly to the majors at Cleveland. I only had to go through it once."

This was a period in Doby's life that revealed much about his upbringing, his character, and why many mistook his silence for belligerence. He wasn't sullen. He was living, until his marriage, a life of total loneliness.

When Larry's father died, his mother had to leave him with relatives. When she brought him to Paterson, she boarded him with different female friends because there was no room for him in her employer's home where she worked as a domestic. And while he certainly had real friends with the Eagles, he had very few within and outside his major-league locker room at first.

That all fits together when you consider what he told his biographer Joe Moore: "I had been alone most of my life. I had gotten accustomed to that. Not that I wanted to be alone. You learn to live with being alone."

When Effa Manley's phone call awakened Doby that morning in 1947, he was on a torrid streak at the plate. He and teammate Monte Irvin were in a dazzling battle for the Negro National League batting title, and Doby was leading the league in home runs. This was where each wanted to be, playing the game they loved in a league of their own—a place where those who saw them play understood how they felt and appreciated what they did. The last thing on Doby's mind was to be treated like a pawn in an environment that didn't want him.

The night after Effa made the deal, the Eagles had a night game in Wilmington, Delaware. The Negro National League had no players association (as Major League Baseball did). The players played when, where, and how often (including exhibition games) the owners wanted. So the Eagles rode their team bus all the way to Delaware, played the game, and took the long ride back to where they had parked their cars. Then Doby drove his Ford convertible another hour back to Paterson.

By the time he arrived, Wednesday night had melted into Thursday. He'd been asleep for almost an hour when the phone rang. The clock on the nightstand read 5:30.

The residue of a sleep he had barely begun turned his voice into a half whisper. "Hello," he croaked.

"This is Mrs. Manley. I have news for you. We sold your contract to Mr. Veeck and the Indians. You need to be there by Sunday. A man named Louis Jones will introduce himself to you before Sunday's doubleheader. We expect you to play in the opener. You can leave for Penn Station with Mr. Jones after the first game. The Indians are in Chicago."

Everybody from the Manleys and Veeck to Louis Jones seemed to have a plan for him—everybody except Doby himself. By his own account, he had little sleep between then and his final Eagles moments. True to Effa's instructions, he met Jones on time, played the first game of the doubleheader and, in his final at-bat for the Eagles, hit the home run that won the game.

Between games as he dressed for the trip, Eagles manager Biz Mackey presented him with a check for fifty dollars and a toilet kit. Everybody wished him well, but seemingly nobody was sure he could make it. Years later, the man who *was* sure told me so. "He was on a train with a man he didn't know to join a group of players he had never met," Monte Irvin said. "But I had no doubt. I was his double-play partner with the Smart Set. I was his teammate with the Eagles.

"He had competitive fire," Irvin added. "He was big and he was strong, and he could hit the ball a ton. Later, when I was with the Giants and he was still with the Indians, the two teams shared a train home, playing exhibition games along the way. We got to Greensboro, North Carolina, before a hostile, redneck crowd. And he hit a ball farther than I thought a man could. I watched it disappear.

"I felt like it was a statement for both of us."

CHAPTER 7

A JOYLESS DRESSING ROOM, CHEERS FOR LARRY BUT "NOT ON MY BLOCK"

When Lou Jones left him at the dressing room entrance, they made plans for Jones to drive him back to the DuSable Hotel after the game. Now Doby stood alone and reached for the door handle. He anticipated the locker room sounds and sights that had been his world since Eastside High School. He turned the handle and walked inside.

It was nothing like he expected. There was the short speech by Boudreau that was more of a preface than an endorsement, followed by the introductions that so many of his new teammates ignored. But then, as Doby recalled for me, "a player reached out and said, 'Hello, Larry. I'm Joe Gordon.'"

You know the rest. The dead-fish handshakes . . . the guys who faced the wall . . . the nightmare season that followed. And there would be the five guys who shook his hand and the calendar that would bring him to "next year."

And when he returned to Paterson in the offseason, he rediscovered something about himself. He realized that he had, in

Helyn Doby, an asset that would emerge as so much more than locker room support. She visited him during the season and, when she was home, was no more than a phone call away. She was always the family CEO.

"During the bad times," he told me when he was re-creating that awful period, "she would never let me bring it home. When I had a bad day at bat or when racial insults hit too hard, she would bring me back to reality with a single phrase: 'It's baseball, honey, and in baseball there is always tomorrow.'"

Casey Stengel could not have said it better.

And that's the way they ran their home. Christina Fearrington, the oldest of five Doby children, explained it best. "They wanted it understood that they were not celebrities, and we were not the bad children of celebrities," she said. "They wanted us to feel that way. Daddy played baseball and he was our father, just like other kids whose fathers might be lawyers or teachers or salesmen. But in baseball season he wasn't there, so unlike other moms she had to run everything, and that included going to school alone when one of us was in a play or had a discipline problem. Running everything about the family was all on her.

"But the great thing about both of them was that they let us be us. They never told us who to go out with or who not to go out with. The friends of all of us were always at our house. It was a kind of meeting place, a house filled with kids of all ages. . . . Because of the difference in the ages of our siblings, everybody had their own friends. Anyone who was respectful was always welcome. When our father was away, she had to be the disciplinarian. She was the one who grounded us, and sometimes when we were really young she delivered the spankings."

Friday had special significance in the Doby house. It was known as "grievance night," in which their five kids were allowed to voice their feelings about discipline they felt was unfair. History does not tell us how many times the elders reversed a decision, but the kids agreed they were appealing to a very tough jury.

"She believed people were people," Doby told Dave Anderson of the *New York Times* for Helyn's obituary. "She believed that when God put people on this earth, it didn't matter what color or nationality He gave them. She believed you had to respect them all. I remember one grievance night she told the kids, 'If you get in trouble with the police, we will help you, but if you get in trouble over drugs, we won't help you.'

"When two of our kids got a little too mischievous, she put them in Catholic school, where the nuns would be more likely to discipline them. If I hadn't married her, I might have had the same success in baseball but never the kind of family life she made possible."

Christina, the first child, would not be born until midseason 1949. So during his disastrous and sometimes racist first season, and during the amazing turnaround of 1948, after Larry went to the outfield, it was Larry and Helyn leaning on and drawing strength from each other, and from friends, in their first apartment in his old Carroll Street neighborhood. They were a constituency whose support did not weaken in the darkest of days.

After the 1948 season . . . the year his home run helped win the World Series . . . the year of the iconic photo with Steve Gromek . . . there was every reason for Larry and Helyn to believe that most of the pressure of his lonely journey to integrate the American League was over. When he returned to Paterson in the offseason following the championship of 1948 with his $6,000 winner's share of the Series, plus a few extra bucks for appearing in the movie *The Kid from Cleveland*, they learned otherwise.

They went house hunting. The exclusive realtors, who sold virtually every home in the area they had chosen, had their own rules. First and foremost, they agreed not to sell to Blacks. Consequently, Larry and Helyn were forced to find a house in a nice area, but not the one they really wanted. Ironically, in making their substitute selection, they found themselves reunited with the residue of the old neighborhood. The immigrant parents of Carroll Street valued education, as most immigrant parents did. They impressed upon their children the notion that "with America's opportunity, you could become a 'somebody.'" When the Dobys arrived in their new neighborhood, Larry's stickball companions from Carroll Street had already taken the advice about education and jobs from their parents and preceded him there.

Just like it had been in the Carroll Street environment, the new one was relatively racist-free, consisting of mostly Jews and some Blacks. As a case in point, one of its attractions was a Chinese restaurant that became a popular family-night-out spot. The owner was a man of obvious Chinese DNA. In keeping with the area's melting-pot population, nobody complained when they discovered he was married to a Jewish woman.

Like their neighbors, the Dobys rarely left the area. All the merchants from grocers to drug stores were right there. The only intrusion of racism for them was when they rode the bus downtown to see a movie and were restricted to the balcony.

But the unapologetic racism the Dobys encountered from real estate agents and biased homeowners—which forced an ad hoc compromise that settled them into the East 27th Street neighborhood, where Larry's boyhood friends had resettled—was never solved. It would return in full force to haunt them as more kids were born and the family's housing needs grew larger. According to a government-funded report on Paterson housing practices in the 1940s, a Black family could finally obtain a sale by paying a white man $1,000 to pretend he was the buyer. When the homeowner did find out, the sale got tied up in court and was nullified.

Racism in Paterson real estate was real and ugly, much like a stubborn case of athlete's foot that occasionally disappeared but repeatedly resurfaced. Finally, in 1960, rebuffed over and over by the usual cabal of homeowners and real estate agents, Larry and Helyn, who had never known another hometown since they met in high school, packed up their Paterson memories and moved to nearby Montclair.

But the finality of that move was well into the future. They chose Montclair because of its progressive educational system and, as Larry Jr. recalled, "we had two aunts living there." It also helped that a number of family friends, including Larry's old Smart Set coach and mentor, Pat Wilson, also lived there. Despite his prestige status as a major-league All-Star and the tsunami of public honors he had achieved over the years in Paterson, the man who broke the American League's color line was denied a home in his own hometown.

Historically, the autumn of 1948 was marked by two significant but opposite events for the Doby family. Larry Doby returned from the Indians' World Series triumph against the Boston Braves, and the city of Paterson, at the direction of its City Council, welcomed him home with a parade in his honor. Cheering Patersonians jammed the parade route. The crowd brought back memories for Larry and Helyn of the days when his all-white high school football teammates not only accepted him but aggressively defended him.

It was the perfect homecoming.

But before the end of the month, while house hunting, they were rebuffed by the other side of the city's old-money families with the phrase "not on our block." Those words would haunt the back roads of his mind forever.

The real estate agents who blocked the sale of the house they wanted most were racists, pure and simple. But they did not represent most of Paterson. In the end, Mayor Michael DeVita, who felt both he and the city of Paterson were embarrassed by Doby's problem, stepped in and negotiated a solution. Both Dobys had seen an alternate selection in a good part of town. It was not the area Helyn wanted, but the compromise was acceptable.

At the end of the year, the mayor insisted that Doby fill a vacancy on the Board of Recreation. It was a face-saving effort to undo the impact of the real estate snub. But Doby's acknowledgment of the appointment was a rare insight into his character.

Ironically, the appointment was offered on a night when Doby, Jackie Robinson, and Roy Campanella were attending a basketball game in New York at the Renaissance Palace that featured the New York Rens, a team which Doby had once received an offer to play for.

Doby told the mayor, "I am very glad to serve because it gives me a chance to do work for the benefit of Paterson's children." That sounds like a cliché, but I can attest to the fact that thirty years later we both served in volunteer jobs with Project Pride, a charity I had founded that sent more than a thousand kids to college.

In February 1949, Larry Doby left for spring training in Tucson, Arizona. If the actions of real estate brokers in his hometown were a surprise, he knew exactly what awaited him in Arizona. Once again, he would be legally barred from sharing the team's hotel with his teammates. Helyn, pregnant with their first child, would also be barred if she came to visit. Ironically, decades later, struggling to avoid public scorn, Arizona claimed the fact that there was no seating segregation at the spring games was to the state's credit as furthering integration. Denial of fair housing and access to public dining apparently didn't count, or perhaps the employees at Randolph Municipal Baseball Park knew that Veeck once pulled a team out of Florida because of segregated seating, and that was the last kind of publicity the Tucson Chamber of Commerce needed.

Mike Veeck remembered it well. "In 1949," he said, "my dad couldn't talk the hotel into letting Larry stay with us, although they did say they would the following year." Talk about promises deferred. That promise wasn't kept until 1965. Until then, Doby stayed at the home of Chester Willis, an employee of the laundry that supplied the towels at the Santa Rita Hotel, where his teammates stayed. The Indians negotiated an agreement by which the Willis family would also supply breakfast and dinner. The home was at 932 Alder Avenue, in the segregated Dunbar School District neighborhood. Satchel Paige, the second Black on the Indians roster, also lived there.

Downtown Tucson was not desegregated, so their social life was limited to the Dunbar neighborhood. In many ways the collective mentality of Arizona clung to its racism all the way to 1991 when, after a bitter fight, National Football League owners took away the state's right to host the 1993 Super Bowl because its legislature would not recognize the birthday of Dr. Martin Luther King Jr. as a legal holiday.

Paul Tagliabue, the NFL commissioner at the time, had struck a blow directly at the bigoted attitude and the same kind of thinking that had earlier sought to make life miserable for Doby. Paul Johnson, the mayor of Phoenix, countered with, "I think the NFL has plenty to apologize for and should be ashamed of their actions."

Tough talk. But it wasn't pro football that blinked. Instead, Phoenix's constituency and big local money couldn't take the chance—they backed off and apologized through a public referendum that enabled the holiday and brought the game there in 1994.

I never got to ask Doby what he thought of what football did for America when it withdrew that game. But I have always wondered what might have happened in the 1940s for Jackie, Larry, and those who followed had baseball cared one scintilla about the segregation of its Black players in their home cities or on the road.

Following their preseason schedule, the Indians and the New York Giants shared a train through the South, playing exhibition games at each stop. Paige and Doby were not close friends, but the Giants had two Black players, Monte Irvin and Hank Thompson, and Monte and Larry had been teammates on the Eagles. So Larry was no longer alone during the long train trip. This was his third season since shattering the American League color line, yet his relationship with most of the Cleveland newspapermen was still tenuous and puzzling.

Cleveland Plain Dealer columnist Gordon Cobbledick had a relationship with Doby that was more of an uneasy truce. In late July, Cobbledick, also the *Plain Dealer*'s sports editor, concluded his column on Doby with an observation: "I earnestly hope that he will blossom into a big leaguer in every sense of the term. I believe the great majority of white fans will give him every possible break."

Cobbledick was a distinguished baseball writer, and he said the right thing at the right time in his column that day. But I am not surprised that he and Doby were not close. The schools were still segregated in Cleveland, and so was the real estate. Lloyd Price, the great R&B singer who spent a lot of time there, once told me that the city's Black and white communities were in so little contact back then that the main factor of friction was less racism and more the ignorance of not knowing what to expect from one another.

Contrast that earlier printed quote with a conversation Doby and Cobbledick had in the dugout before Opening Day in 1949. Doby's awkward debut was long since over. The second year (1948) was honeymoon—the team's first World Series championship in twenty-eight years. And now it was the third season.

Cobbledick was sitting in the home dugout two hours before game time when he motioned Doby over and started a conversation.

"You had a great year," the columnist said. "Does that mean you're going to take the shield down?"

Puzzled, Doby responded, "I don't know what you mean."

Conclusion: Neither of them did.

Cobbledick, like most in his profession, had never covered a Black baseball player fighting for acceptance until Doby came to Cleveland, and Doby hadn't been covered by a white sportswriter since high school. Neither man understood the route the other had traveled. No local writer had a frame of reference to understand how the years of loneliness had impacted Doby. Or how years debating things like the designated hitter rule came between baseball and human understanding.

This was why that single one-sentence conversation between Doby and Cobbledick was confusing to both men. To Cobbledick, Doby's caution around writers came off as moodiness and a touch of racism. To Doby, experience told him to be careful, to wait for the other shoe to drop, because with his seasoning he was sure it would. The writers who then covered Doby took a long time to take the shield down, as did Larry himself.

Much later, Cobbledick would write an article for *Sport* magazine titled, "Is Larry Doby a Bust?"

But by then there was no relationship—shield up or down. It worsened late in Doby's playing career with a rash of leg injuries so frequent that he hired track star Harrison Dillard to live with him in the offseason one winter to help him try to get into shape. When Cobbledick wrote that Doby was a loner and a messed-up guy who blamed race for every problem, Doby shot back that pitchers were throwing at Black hitters too often. Nobody in the major press corps agreed. Then Sam Lacy, the talented sports editor of the *Baltimore Afro-American*, did the homework. He claimed that the eight Black players in both leagues by then were hit 68 times. That's 8.5 times per man. No white player was hit as many as eight times all season.

Cobbledick was not the only Cleveland writer who had difficulty understanding Doby. After the 1955 season, in which Doby had 26 home runs and 75 RBIs while hitting .291 in

131 games, his fewest played since 1948, he was traded to the Chicago White Sox for outfielder Jim Busby and infielder Chico Carrasquel. Franklin Lewis, a columnist for the *Cleveland Press,* wrote, "He has been a controversial athlete. Highly gifted, he was frequently morose, sullen, and upon occasion downright surly to his teammates. . . . He thought of himself, at the beginning, as the symbol of the Negro in his league." Lewis thought he had figured out that somehow race was involved in the way he and others perceived Larry's attitude. On that he was correct, but the problem was generated by the way the only Black American Leaguer was treated from the moment he stepped into a world that was snowy white. Lewis had neither the depth nor the social experience to understand what he saw as "attitude."

Eventually, in 1951 and 1952, the unfair war between Doby, the victim, and Cobbledick and Lewis, the bullies, accelerated to the point where both writers were precariously balanced on a tightrope stretched between selective criticism and undisguised racism. According to Joe Moore in his biography of Doby, Lewis once wrote, "Doby, already wearing the shield of the Negro on his nameplate, withdrew into a mental dungeon." And Cobbledick contributed, "He is a friendless loner, presided over by his attractive wife, Helyn, and dominated by his two-year-old daughter."

I have been a newspaperman for seventy-two years. I can recall the days when the mores of the time almost always identified Blacks by race in the daily papers. But no matter how harsh the criticism, I never read such blatant personal racism, except from the bottom-feeders who populate some shameless internet sites today.

Ironically, there was one strong human emotion during that time that remained with Doby decades later. It had nothing to do with the hostile teammates who insulted him in the beginning, or writers who never understood him (nor cared to try). It was the biggest single saving grace he would never forget: the fans. He was sitting on the couch with Larry Doby Jr., watching a Yankees-Red Sox game on TV, when a player booted a grounder. The home crowd erupted with a torrent of boos. The elder Doby turned to his son and, summoning up a long-gone era of a great recollection in a time that did not produce a lot of them, said simply, "They never booed me in Cleveland."

Baseball had unleashed a serious memory that overrode a slew of bad ones.

The 1949 major-league All-Star Game was played at Ebbets Field in Brooklyn. This was where Jackie Robinson had sat in the office of Branch Rickey and signed his first contract with the Dodgers organization. But he gave that little thought before this game, when he dutifully lined up for pregame photos with three other All-Stars on the dugout steps.

Like the Doby-Gromek picture snapped during the World Series a year earlier, this was iconic. The first one, a white man and a Black man hugging in mutual celebration, was history because it had never happened. Neither had this one—four superheroes, who happened to be Black, chosen for this classic game between the two leagues. No Black man had ever been in an All-Star dugout before. Three years earlier it would have been an impossible dream in the hearts and minds of the four. They each posed with one foot on the steps and one in the dugout. They were hardly strangers to one another. Roy Campanella, Don Newcombe, and Jackie Robinson—all of them Dodgers—and Larry Doby from the Indians.

All four had been signed off Negro League rosters, but Doby was the only one whom baseball general managers had paid to sign; Rickey and the Dodgers refused to negotiate or pay for their three. Veeck, of course, paid the Eagles for Doby. The Dodgers' contingent was voted in as All-Star starters. Doby, who was appointed as a reserve, had an off year—for him. He hit .280 with 25 doubles, 85 RBIs, 106 runs scored, and 24 home runs. Though his batting average was a slump for him, the doubles runs scored were a tribute to his speed on the bases.

The home runs spoke for themselves.

CHAPTER 8

THURSDAY'S CHILD AND A HURT IN LARRY'S HEART

Larry Doby hit .326 in 1950, along with 25 home runs. And he majestically swept across center field as though he had a chattel mortgage on every blade of grass. His natural ability masked the pain in his legs. Nobody could explain it. Nobody could pinpoint how it first came or why it sporadically disappeared or why it always came back—not the trainers, not the doctors, not even Harrison Dillard, the four-time Olympic gold-medal sprinter and hurdler who worked for the Indians and actually moved in with Doby one offseason to work on conditioning.

Doby fought through the pain, spurred on by the knowledge that for a Black man to be accepted as a major leaguer in that era, "just as good" wasn't good enough. He had to be better. In 1949, he had been reunited with his old Mogmog buddy from World War II, Mickey Vernon, the respected big leaguer who had risked his own career lobbying Washington Senators owner Clark Griffith to sign Doby. (If you wonder why it was such a risk for a white player to ask his boss to sign a Black one, then consider the remarks of Calvin Griffith, the son and heir, when he moved the team to Minneapolis: "I'll tell you why we came to Minnesota. It was when we found out you only had 15,000 Black people here. Black people don't go to ballgames, but they'll fill up a wrestling ring and put up such a chant it'll scare you to death. We came here because you've got good, hardworking white people here.")

That friendship between Doby and Vernon lasted long after baseball, but in mid-June 1950 Vernon was traded back to Washington after he was replaced at first base by Luke Easter. Doby lost a friend and teammate that day but gained a roommate. Satchel Paige was gone, released before spring training. The team's road secretary paired Easter and Doby in places where hotels would not let Blacks stay with the rest of the team. They were roommates for a little less than six seasons. Not close friends, but with a great appreciation of the characteristics that shaped their individual and often opposite personalities.

Doby was the consummate professional, playing with dedicated intensity as his own legitimate toughest critic when he felt he did not live up to his own standards. Luke Easter did not come from the kind of baseball background that produced Doby. Easter came to baseball late. His youth was spent shining shoes, apprenticed to a guy who made hats, and another who owned a dry-cleaning establishment. Nothing about his personality resembled the little boy with the baseball glove that once was Larry Doby. While their two personalities were so different, their paths to the big leagues were carbon-copy parallel. Like Doby and the Smart Set, Easter began his career with a sandlot team called the Cincinnati Crescents and then morphed into the Negro National League with the powerful Homestead Grays.

Like Doby, his contract was purchased by Bill Veeck. Yet the similarities ended there.

Veeck optioned Easter to San Diego in the Pacific Coast League, where he batted .363 and slammed 25 home runs. A decade before Doby fought a personal segregation war as the only Black man in the American League, the PCL had already integrated its teams and hotels in which they stayed. Race, therefore, presented no barrier for him when he joined San Diego. But it became one in mid-August 1949, when the Indians recalled him. He was for that brief time Doby's roommate, and by spring training of 1950 the arrangement became permanent. They became the Indians' odd couple. At first, Doby thought Easter's approach to both life and the game was his polar opposite—which was why it worked. It proved to be a caring counterbalance to his roommate's intensity.

Easter was a well-worn thirty-four-year-old rookie when they first met. Reality drove them together. The rules had yet to change for Doby, and they were brand new for Easter. As Black men with talent, they were accorded a seat in the dugout, a spot in the batting order, and a clear understanding of where they better not eat, sleep, or socialize. More easily summed up as "Hit the ball, mind your own business, and stay invisible."

It was far easier for Larry because this was his fourth Major League season. He had been tested by fire and emerged by then as an established All-Star. Easter was stepping into baseball segregation for the first time; it was not the way race worked in the PCL. Ironically, while Doby guided him through the first two rules, it was the third one that killed his promising career. He was cheated out of his place in the game's history by the fact that he was born too soon and too Black.

Doby survived off a blend of sheer talent, determination, and the chiding, understanding, and unwavering love of Helyn Curvy Doby. Except for his power as a hitter, Luke Easter had nothing resembling Larry's familial support. But nobody challenged the fact that he could hit the ball. He was 6-foot-4 and weighed 240 pounds, with the dimensions of the Ambrose Lightship. His name was Lucious, but he never used it. Built the way he was, it was no wonder he didn't have to repeat himself when he'd say, "Call me Luke."

"They still talk about the ball he hit in Cleveland's Municipal Stadium," Larry Jr. told me. "It landed 447 feet from home plate. The longest ball ever hit there. I climbed to the upper deck to see where it landed. I couldn't believe anybody could hit a baseball that far."

The truth is that Easter hit at least one even farther. It happened in the Polo Grounds when Easter's Negro American League team played a game there. Nobody ever hit a ball into the center-field bleachers there until Easter clocked one 475 feet from home plate. Only Lou Brock and Joe Adcock ever duplicated that feat.

"If he had a weakness," Doby told me about Easter, "it was cards. One night, he and Suitcase Simpson and Sam Jones were playing Spades High, so I went to the movies. Luke drew the ace of spades 21-straight times. On the 22nd deal, the ace of spades fell out of his sleeve. When I got back, Easter was on my side of the door with a chair in his hands. Sam was on the other side with a broken beer bottle. But they made up the next day. You couldn't stay mad at Luke. He was a beautiful person. There was nothing he wouldn't do for you.

"But my biggest memory of Luke is also my saddest. It was the last day of the 1952 season and we were tied for the home run title.

I hit my 32nd early that day. Now it was his last time at bat, and he desperately wanted that swing. But they walked him—and he froze and he just stood there saying it wasn't fair. And he wouldn't move. The umpire, Charley Berry, tried to tell him he had to go down to first but he still didn't move. He said it wasn't right. He wanted a piece of that title so badly. It was like he knew what was going to happen. It was like he knew he'd never get another shot. Of course, he didn't know. It took 10 minutes, but finally he went down to first. But it was like he could look into the future."

You could make a case that he could, and did. The "girlfriend" thing exploded—and it sent him to the minors the following year.

"That made no sense," Doby told me. "Here's a man who hit 31 home runs that season, and drove in a ton of runs, and they still ship him back down. It puzzles me."

But it really didn't. He knew exactly why. So did everyone else on the Indians. He knew that what pushed Luke to the minors would not have generated so much as a stare today. Doby wanted to tell the story in his old roomie's defense, but he never identified the racist players who pressured management to get rid of him.

"He had a white girlfriend," Doby said. "She sat right behind first base. Two or three of our teammates didn't like it and said so over and over. The man hit 31 home runs and they sent him down. We all knew why, and whose complaints were behind it."

Every time the two of us spoke about Easter, I thought about a nursery rhyme, the one that begins *Monday's child is fair of face and Tuesday's child is full of grace. . . .* The one that includes *Thursday's child has far to go. . . .*

It is self-evident that you had to be there to understand how complicated the Thursday child named Luke Easter was. Larry knew because he was there to share it as no other member of that team, with the possible exception of Al Rosen, a Jew born in the South, who years after Luke was out of baseball hired him to be a coach for a few games to make him eligible for his baseball pension. Except for this last headline, Big Luke fell off the map and into obscurity until we spoke of him at the end of his life. The bigots who complained about Easter got rid of him off a myth. There never has been a correlation between how many home runs a man with Easter's power could have hit for the Indians and who was his bed partner.

He went down to the minors, to Triple-A Rochester and Buffalo, and wham . . . bam . . . damn . . . he hit the cover off the ball. It was as though he was hammering out a simple message: "If they playin' baseball, I don't need no major league salary. Just shut up and pitch." In those days, a successful minor-league team brought prestige to smaller cities, and its home run hero was idolized. Luke Easter didn't just hit home runs, he hit ballistic missiles, and they were respectfully called "Easter Eggs."

And then he quit. Doby lost track of him.

Until . . .

On a spring day in 1979, I was in the office when the story came over the Associated Press wire. The day before, as Luke Easter had done once a week for years, he went down to the bank in Euclid, Ohio, to cash his check and those of his co-workers from the TRW plant where he worked as a polisher and was the shop steward. He cashed $5,000 in checks and left. Two men cornered him in the bank parking lot and demanded the money. One had a shotgun, the other a .38-caliber. When Easter refused, they opened fire simultaneously. Easter never had a chance. He died on the way to the hospital.

It wasn't easy telling Doby over the telephone.

There was a long pause, followed by a single moan of a word: "Damn . . ." followed by another pause.

Doby finally spoke. "He was a good human being. We went through a lot together."

He took it like a death in the family.

The local media was scapegoating him for the failure of the Indians to get back to the World Series. It was easier for baseball writers to focus blame on a single Black man than to dig into the failures of the front office.

I did not know it at the time, but in talking about the 1950 All-Star Game, Larry Doby Jr. casually gave me a clue to the silent depth of the bond between his dad and Luke Easter. That was the game in which Ted Williams, often criticized by Boston writers as mediocre in the field, crashed into the scoreboard in the first inning while catching a line drive by Ralph Kiner. The wall was cement and Williams fractured his left elbow.

Doby had a late flight out of Chicago the next day. He wanted to visit Williams in the hospital, with good reason. Williams had continually told him to keep his chin up, that he had the talent to be a superstar. Apparently, Easter was either told or sensed this. He told Larry he wanted to go with him to the hospital.

They were the only players who visited Williams.

At the funeral home in Cleveland, four thousand fans filed past Easter's casket for a last look at their hero; at Mount Sinai Baptist Church, more than a thousand people attended the funeral; Cleveland police led a procession of 150 cars to the cemetery. In the casket was a fresh deck of Luke's favorite "Bee" playing cards, placed there by his son, Gerald.

Despite the pain in his legs, Doby was chosen to his second All-Star Game that year; he made it a total of seven times during his big-league career. In later years, it was thought he might have developed a degenerative bone disease. But in 1983, at age sixty, he played in the Cracker Jack Old-Timers Baseball Classic in Washington, and Larry Doby Jr. recalled, "I never realized how fast he was until that day. He hit a bang-banger to the deep infield, and he almost beat the throw."

The Indians finished 30 games above .500 in 1950 (92–62), but wound up in fourth place. Much of the local media continued to blame him for the fact that they had not won the World Series since 1948, when his bat had been the primary reason they did. But the blame may have again been racially motivated, as he led the team in batting average (.326), on-base percentage (.442), slugging (.545), hits (164), and runs (110). He would also finish eighth in MVP voting.

There seemed to be light at the end of the tunnel at last for the Doby family. In the spring of 1954, Larry reported to camp with his best financial contract: a $28,000 salary, the highest of his career, a long way from the Manleys and their $300 a month. Management finally understood what Larry brought to every pennant chase: power at the plate, speed despite his aching legs. He also brought a special quality to this team—a fierce desire to win that was highly contagious. From a talented but silent teammate, he had morphed into a force both in the locker room and on the field.

Now there was financial breathing room for Helyn to manage the family. She was perfect for the job. When she was growing up in the Curvy house, there were ten siblings, three bedrooms, and three beds: one for the boys, one for the girls, one for the parents.

"You could wake up with somebody's foot in your face," she told Junior once in a rare conversation about her own girlhood and her responsibility as the chief babysitter.

"When my dad passed," Junior said, "I could still go on the internet and see him and try to understand what he went through, but not my mom. I wanted to sit her down and record her memories on videotape, but she refused. They both always agreed on what they would and would not tell us. I was the only boy, and my dad was not going to tell me how bad it was for him until I got older. When I got my scholarship to Duke, he was over the moon. I think he wanted me to leave baseball behind when I got my degree because he knew what college could do for me. But he never interfered. There's a story about that.

"We were on the telephone, and I told him I'd just met my baseball coach. He didn't know it was Enos Slaughter, the old St. Louis Cardinal who was alleged to have planned a strike when they got to Brooklyn and Mr. Robinson walked out on the field. I had no idea how dad would react. And then he said it doesn't matter whether he liked dad or dad liked him. What matters, he insisted, was how coach and I liked each other. He said people grow. That thing with Mr. Robinson was a long time ago.

"And then he might go to the All-Star Game and see coach there, and when he came home he would always say, 'I saw your coach there and he said to tell you hello.' That, for me, was a teachable moment because both of them were always there for me."

But there was more to the story that Junior did not know. On June 13, 1957, Doby was playing for the White Sox in a game against the Yankees. Art Ditmar, a journeyman pitcher then with the Yanks, did what pitchers always do when faced with a power hitter who was trying to crowd the plate: he threw one high and tight. Doby wasn't hit, but a few seconds later the ball got away and the catcher chased it to keep a run from scoring.

Ditmar raced in to cover the plate. Doby said something, Ditmar said something, and then Doby flattened him with a left hook. As Doby recalled it for me, he remembered Yankee Moose Skowron jumping on his back, and then he saw Walt Dropo, the big Chicago first baseman, leading the Sox out of their dugout to defend him and heading straight for Skowron.

"I had to laugh," Doby said. "Eleven years in the league and now I finally got teammates." What he never told Junior was that coming out of the Yankees dugout, in time to get kicked out of the game along with Doby, was Enos Slaughter, Junior's future coach at Duke.

"Hey," Larry told me, "it wasn't racism. It was just baseball."

It wasn't race. It was the eternal battle between pitcher and hitter. It was the residue of a fierce pennant fight between the league-leading White Sox and the pursuing New York Yankees. The day before, Yankees pitcher Al Cicotte had twice sent Chicago left fielder Minnie Minoso sprawling in the dirt; at game's end, Minoso had to be restrained when he went after Cicotte.

What it was, in fairness to everyone, was perfectly explained by the erudite *Washington Post* columnist Shirley Povich: "This is no attempt to condone what Doby did; merely to point out the consequences fell far short of civil war, secession or a violent sense of outrage except for teammates that dashed to his assistance but no more in anger than had he been a white player. In a strange but honest way Doby had been in a headline not as a Black baseball player but as a typical baseball player."

Povich told it like it was and like baseball needed to hear. But not Helyn. When Junior asked her how bad those times were, she told him, "If you keep talking about it, then it becomes a bigger problem, and your mind will become hateful." But she knew the score. She knew everything her husband endured.

She was there in the stands and she heard it all, the cries of "Nigger!" and "Boy!" and a lot worse. But she was prepared because segregation wasn't new to her—even in the North. In Paterson, as kids, she and Larry had to sit in the movie theater balcony or they couldn't go. It hurt a lot more in the American League cities, this being baseball, America's game.

One day, long after Doby left baseball, Helyn was complaining about a bad call she thought an umpire had made the night before during a televised game. Larry laughed and stared at her across the breakfast table. "When did you become a baseball expert?" Then she said, "Well, you read the paper from the sports in the back to the front. But you never get to the front. I read it from the front, and I always get to the sports in the back. Yes, he made a bad call." When Doby told me that story, he laughed and said, "We started together as kids, as first loves. Nothing ever changed that."

There was a powerful message in that, and Helyn never forgot it. Junior recalled the day Helyn was watching television and heard a player's wife say, "I am gonna be more than just a player's wife."

"Mom was furious," Junior said. "'More than just a player's wife? Who keeps the family together? Who pays the bills during the season? Who raises the player's kids when he can't be there?

"'More than just a player's wife,'" she repeated angrily. "'That woman has no idea what she is talking about.'"

CHAPTER 9

THE BEST DAMN PITCHERS IN BASEBALL, THE CATCH, AND THE EMBARRASSMENT

In 1954, Doby reported to spring training with a justifiable new optimism, no doubt boosted by the numbers in his new contract. A year earlier, the pain in his legs seemed to ease. He hit 29 home runs and driven in 102 runs while making his fifth consecutive All-Star Game appearance. In '54, he would hit 32 homers and knock in 126; Al Rosen, the talented third baseman, would hit .300 with 24 homers and 102 RBIs; and second baseman Bobby Ávila suddenly had become the hottest hitter on the team with a surprising .341 average, the highest in the American League.

Doby's new $28,000 salary took the pressure off on the home front. It doesn't sound like much, but in today's market it would be worth more than $311,000. Additionally, Helyn Doby had settled into life as a baseball player's wife relatively free from distractions. Where acceptance by the community of wives was all but impossible when Doby first got to the big leagues, she now had a warm circle of friends, including the wives of Jim

Hegan, Bob Lemon, Joe Gordon, and Steve Gromek. They were joined by the wife of newcomer Mike Garcia.

Spring training hotels in Arizona were still a year away from integration, but Helyn and the other players' wives were fully integrated in their social activities. There was an interesting parallel here with Rachel Robinson, Jackie's wife, who even earlier had been welcomed by the Dodgers' wives.

"I don't remember the guy's name, I was too young, but there was a player he didn't like and who didn't like him," Junior recalled. "It was a home game. That night my dad asked her who she went to the game with that day and she named the player's wife and added, 'We had a great time.' My dad just shook his head and walked away. Each of them always took people as they found them. They were very strong-minded people."

The Indians had improved, and when Doby joined them in Tucson that February there was clear optimism in camp. Rosen had hit 43 home runs the previous season and won the American League MVP; additionally, despite the decline of Bob Feller, they began to build what a year later would be the best pitching staff in all of baseball.

But Doby in '53 was in the middle of what for his talent was considered a so-so season. While he hit 29 home runs and drove in 102 runs, his batting average slumped to .263—while also leading the American League in strikeouts, with 126—reigniting the old scorn of Franklin Lewis and Gordon Cobbledick, who blamed him in part for their inability to catch the Yankees. They finished in second place by eight and a half games. It was a long winter in the Doby household.

In the wake of that alleged failure, neither Lewis nor Cobbledick had the slightest idea that this team would simultaneously sandwich the greatest American League season in history with one of the greatest all-time failures.

Overall, the balance was better than ever. And the pitching? Well, it was the best in all of baseball, and as Doby told me, "It made the hitting better and the hitters more relaxed. They took the pressure off me and Rosen. If we hit a home run with a guy on base, it was generally all our pitchers needed. And we hit a lot home runs as a team that year."

The real story was 60 feet, six inches from home plate. There were three future Hall of Famers: Early Wynn, Bob Lemon, and Bob Feller, whose spectacular career was finally in decline. Lemon was best at 23–7, followed by Wynn at 23–11; Mike Garcia was 19–8, Art Houtteman 15–7, and the less-used Feller was 13–3.

Among this group, surprisingly, Wynn was the most feared—and with good reason. I once heard him say, "There is the batter's box and there's home plate. And then there's about one to two inches on the border. They belong to me. You better stay out of there." Nobody ever enforced that edict better than Wynn, and what made him so effective was that hitters knew it.

On paper, it could have been the greatest pitching staff ever assembled going into a World Series. Unfortunately, they don't play for championships on paper.

So the Cleveland Indians thought they were back in business. Nobody in the Cleveland media could find a single ax, or even a Boy Scout penknife, to grind against the home team. About 1.3 million fans poured through the Municipal Stadium turnstiles. And the best of all possible worlds for them was the fact that the hated New York Yankees were a full eight games back. It was 1948 all over again, they thought, but this time it wouldn't even be close. They were witnesses to the oldest cliché in baseball: "Great pitching will always beat great hitting."

Through a season almost devoid of drama, there came a single moment of Larry Doby on display that might have been the greatest catch that nobody remembers in the history of baseball. It was preceded by the All-Star Game on July 13. He was the backup center fielder on the American League roster, and pinch-hit the home run that tied the game. At season's end, he finished second to Yogi Berra in the AL MVP voting.

Seventeen days later, the Indians took the Larry Doby Thrill Show into the nation's capital and Griffith Stadium, against the hapless Washington Senators in the first of a four-game series. The Senators were headed nowhere and would finish 22 games under .500.

With a man on first and weak-hitting Tom Umphlett at bat, Doby was playing fairly deep, something of a surprise considering that Umphlett was hitting all of .217. Doby backpedaled toward the center-field fence—this was not an ordinary fly ball from a guy barely hitting over .200.

To everyone in the stadium, it looked as though Doby was headed for a dangerous collision, but at the last second he seemed to kangaroo straight up in the air, his glove higher than the fence. Doby made the catch. As he came down, his leg went through the awning over the bullpen. Outfielder Al Smith had run with him, and as Doby lay motionless on the ground Smith plucked the ball out of Doby's glove and fired it to the relay man. The baserunners could not score.

Just to put the cherry on top of this baseball version of a hot-fudge sundae, Doby hit his 21st homer in the fifth inning. The old pitcher Dizzy Dean summed it up in the *Cleveland Press* the next day: "I've seen them all—Moore, DiMaggio and this here fellow Mays. But I never saw a catch as good as this one. The pitcher ought to pay that Doby a month's salary."

The "new-look" Indians triggered a justifiable arrogance among the locals. The record-setting games won (111), the tremendous firepower of this once-in-a-lifetime pitching staff, and the torrid pace they set all season had turned the hated Yankees' perennial dominance into a footing based on shifting sands. Doby and Rosen provided the power, and the fact that the World Series opponent was the "other" New York team made the prospects even more intriguing.

The fact that the first game was at New York's Polo Grounds meant nothing to the pundits and the Cleveland faithful. The composite stats were all the evidence fans and bookmakers alike needed. They showed the difference. The Giants were good, but the Indians were great. The Giants were considered what gamblers called an "out bet."

In the very first inning of the first game, the Indians took charge. They scored two off Sal Maglie, the Giants' best pitcher. Leadoff hitter Al Smith was hit by a pitch. Bobby Avila singled, and Vic Wertz scored both with a triple. The Giants tied it in the third. From there to the eighth, the scoreboard showed a string of zeroes. In the top of the eighth, Doby and Rosen singled, and Maglie was replaced by Don Liddle to face Wertz, who the Indians had traded for earlier in the year. He could play the outfield or first base, but it was his reputation as a clutch hitter that finalized the deal. This felt as though it was the moment for which Cleveland had pursued the trade.

What happened next, Doby told me years later, was the beginning, middle, and end of the 1954 Cleveland Indians. "You could feel the air going out of our dugout," he remembered.

It was Wertz against Willie Mays and center field.

Willie won.

The center-field wall at the old Polo Grounds was the furthest from home plate of any center field in the history of the majors—483 feet from the batter's box. There was so much green out there, you'd swear you could raise cattle. On a personal note, I was discharged from the Army in September 1953 after serving in the Korean theater. I was back at the paper, but I was not covering the game—I was sitting in the right-center-field bleachers. I was with my cousin (who bought the tickets as a belated birthday gift) on a busman's holiday. I saw it all up close and personal.

Wertz, a left-handed hitter, made a picture-perfect swing and caught the ball right on the bat's sweet spot. As it rose, I swear it seemed as though it were headed across the river to Yankee Stadium in the Bronx. Out in center, Mays turned his back and began to run. Run? Hell, it looked as though he was jet propelled. The ball climbed higher. Willie ran. The ball kept climbing. Willie ran faster. With his back to home plate, he reached out near the wall and made an incredible over-the-shoulder catch, spun around, and in the same motion hit the cutoff man at the edge of the infield. Nobody scored. They were still on base when the inning ended.

Drama? More of a prelude. They went past the eighth, past the ninth, still tied in the 10th.

Then, with two Giants on base, Dusty Rhodes came out of the dugout to hit for right-handed Monte Irvin. Dusty had come to the Giants after a five-year career in the minors—Hopkinsville,

Hutchinson, Springfield, Des Moines, Grand Rapids, Rock Hill, Nashville—Class C to Triple A. He always had his suitcase packed. The scouting report when the Giants bought his contract in 1952 should have read *Good power. Mediocre fielding and great staying power nightly at any local watering holes for as long as they left the lights on.*

During the 1954 regular season with the Giants, he produced 15 home runs when he platooned with or hit for Irvin. With the odds and the pitching against the Giants, if there were no Dusty Rhodes, they would have had to invent one.

Rhodes hit a soft fly ball to the comfortably close right field wall—258 feet. The ball barely cleared the wall. Willie's catch would have been a home run in Cleveland—and Dusty's home run would have been a popup in Cleveland. Game One absolutely traumatized the Indians. When Rhodes's gamer narrowly topped the right-field wall, Indians pitcher Bob Lemon hurled his glove at the mound in frustration. "The glove went further than the ball I hit," Rhodes quipped.

Lemon was not the first visiting pitcher to be both humiliated and infuriated by the treacherous dimensions of that right-field Polo Grounds wall. It was the comfort zone of every .200 left-handed hitter on every visiting team. Sooner or later, all of us who ever covered the Giants heard the story of the Brooklyn Dodgers relief pitcher who was beaten on a dink home run just like that and who allegedly said after the game, "How far away is that wall? How can they allow it? I could stand on the pitcher's mound and piss over it."

"The season had been so easy and now this," Doby noted. "We talked off and on for years about that series. I know it's hard to believe, but the ball Wertz hit was a home run in our park. And the ball Rhodes hit was a pop fly in our park. And I really believed, even with our good pitching, they broke our spirits." He talked about it so often it was almost like he was still groping for an explanation. It was a Series he wished he could forget. After all the runs he drove home in the regular season, his World Series stat line was a shock: 16 at-bats, two hits . . . a Series batting average of .125 . . . zero runs batted in.

He might have been right about the impact of the Mays catch. After all, the Indians' team batting average for the Series was an atrocious .190, scoring just nine runs to the Giants' 21.

Game Two: Rhodes, pinch-hitting for Irvin, had an RBI single and a late home run. The Giants won it with just four hits, and Dusty had half of them.

Game Three: Cleveland limped home. An incredible crowd of 71,555 turned out to see their miracle comeback. Unfortunately, the only miracle they saw was that the Indians got all of four hits. The Giants' Ruben Gomez was brilliant, and the Indians lost, 6–2. The team that finished 14 wins better than their World Series counterparts were now a game from elimination.

Game Four: Already leading 3–0, the Giants broke it open with a four-run fifth. Dusty Rhodes did not hit a home run; you can't hit one if you don't get in the game. Irvin played all the way and had a two-run single. The season that began with "look what we did" ended with the sound of silence. Even the pigeons off Lake Erie went home early.

Asked to explain Rhodes's World Series performance, Giants' manager Leo Durocher said it was no mystery. "He thinks he is the greatest hitter in the world and this year he was," Durocher said. "Every time during the season when we needed him, he always stepped up." The man who had all of six at-bats had two dingers and seven RBIs, almost outscoring the entire Indians team.

Rhodes's own post–World Series explanation of his fireworks kept it even simpler. He was, after all, anxious to get back into the "neon sunshine," where he was a regular nightly visitor. The team joke was that "he meets himself coming into the hotel after a night out, says hello, showers, and gets on the team bus. He gets off and then hits a home run." That was pretty much his 1954 baseball year. The sudden trip into the World Series spotlight didn't bother Dusty for a single moment: "Some people can play ball this time of year. Others can drink this time of year. I can do both."

The following season, Doby brought a new motivation to preseason camp. He was still frustrated by the way the Giants pitchers held him in check several months earlier. Although his numbers got him chosen to the All-Star Game for the seventh time, the old nagging injuries kept him on the bench. He played the fewest games in his career (131) other than his rookie year (121). Nevertheless, he hit 26 home runs and batted .291, but drove in just 75 runs—his fewest since 1951. At season's end, after nine years in Cleveland, he was traded to the White Sox for Chico Carrasquel and Jim Busby. Chicago was a team starved for power.

Said Chicago manager Marty Marion, "That's why we made the deal for him. The guy used to murder us when he played in Cleveland. He'll make a big difference in one- and two-run decisions we might lose." Marion was right. Doby hit 24 home runs with 102 RBIs in his first season on the South Side, and led the team to a third-place finish. The following season, he tied for the team lead in home runs with 14 and hit .288. The Sox improved to second place.

Doby's earlier sendoff from Cleveland was "celebrated" in a valedictory by Franklin Lewis in the *Plain Dealer*. His farewell to the American League's first Black man ignored the racist way in which most of his new 1947 teammates greeted him; ignored his team-leading batting average in his first full season while learning to play the outfield; ignored his World Series home run that year when the Indians won their first Series title in twenty-eight years. It made no mention of his seven All-Star Game selections.

Instead, Lewis grabbed his readers by the throat as if to say, "All right, fans of the Cleveland Indians, here is what I know about the real inner Larry Doby."

"He had been a controversial athlete. Highly gifted, he was frequently morose, sullen and, upon occasion, downright surly to his teammates. . . . He thought of himself, at the beginning, as the symbol of the Negro in his league." Wrong. He wasn't the symbol in the year of which Lewis wrote. He was the *only* one.

Doby's rebuttal: "I was looked upon as a Black man (that first year), not as a human being. I did feel a responsibility to the Black players who came after me, but that was basically to people, not just to Black people."

A far more accurate rebuttal might have been exactly what he said previously in this book to his son while they watched a game on TV together when the home-team Yankees were booed by their own fans: "They never booed me in Cleveland."

In a man-on-the-street interview (likewise, as noted earlier in the book) after Indians owner Bill Veeck had signed the first Black man in the American League, the response was one of hope rather than racism:

Question: "What do you think of Bill Veeck signing a Negro?" Answer from the fan: "Can he hit? That's all that matters, isn't it?"

That might have been the first time, but surely not the last, in which the fans knew more than the writers.

From the moment Larry Doby joined the Newark Eagles of the Negro National League under an assumed name in 1942, he played baseball for one and only one reason. Like all the players in the Negro Leagues, he played because the game was part of his life. Like a grizzly coming out of hibernation, each spring calendar for him, whether in the Negro Leagues or the American League, was preordained. Apart from his family, there was little else he thought of after nine years in Cleveland. But now a shadow began to blur what had always been a predictable future. Once, shin splints, pulled muscles, and leg pain had been negated by his athletic youth. Now approaching his mid-thirties, the youth was gone and the pain was a far more formidable adversary. Once spring training meant Tucson followed by 154 games against the same seven American League franchises. But even though he was still in the AL, he began to understand that this season it might still be Chicago, or who knew where? And for how long?

Larry did not involve his family. Helyn kept her silence.

But for the first time since he carried that fielder's glove as a little boy in Camden, he realized this was what baseball was all about: a lot was promised, but for how long?

CHAPTER 10

SO WHERE DID YOU GO, LARRY DOBY? JUST ABOUT EVERYWHERE

In late December of 1955, roughly a year after the Great World Series Embarrassment, Santa Claus went AWOL in the Doby house. Helyn realized that in February she would be leaving behind her closest friends among the wives and girlfriends of the Cleveland Indians and heading for Glendale, Arizona, where the Chicago White Sox trained.

And for the first time since that July afternoon in 1947, when more than half of his new teammates in Cleveland refused to shake his hand, Larry Doby would be a stranger in a new locker room. The only familiar face would be the new Chicago manager, Al Lopez, who had been Larry's field boss the previous season in Cleveland. And for the first time in nearly a decade, both husband and wife faced a spring of prospects unknown.

Neither was thrilled. But Larry found some solace in the words of White Sox vice president Chuck Comiskey: "We dealt for Doby because we desperately needed a power hitter." Doby would not disappoint him. He hit 24 home runs and drove in

102 in his first season, and was a serious factor in their third-place finish. A year later, in 1957, he hit .288 but slipped to 14 home runs in just 119 games. The drop in power production coupled with more leg problems sent him an undeniable message. Like all injured and aging ballplayers, at thirty-three years of age, he was becoming just another name in future deals. He did not have to wait long for confirmation.

The Sox dropped him into a multiplayer deal with the Orioles in December 1957. Before the end of spring training, he was shipped back to the Indians in another multiplayer trade. Then a year later it was Detroit (for Tito Francona, whom he had been previously traded to the Orioles for), and then back to Chicago two months later. In 1956, Jackie Robinson was traded to the New York Giants but retired rather than finish his career with the Dodgers' most bitter rival. The writers understood that. They saw it as an affirmation of his New York state of mind, chip-on-the-shoulder attitude. They were probably right. Out of baseball but emotionally still the fighter, Robinson carried on a verbal battle for baseball to hire a Black manager. He did not live long enough to see it happen.

Doby did not walk away until 1960. Instead, he went to San Diego's Pacific Coast League team to try and play his way back to "The Show." But when sliding into third to stretch a double into a triple in a game against Sacramento, his left ankle crumbled.

X-rays showed bone deterioration, yet he tried to soldier on. It wasn't a need for adoration that drove him—it was the last-ditch attempt of the boy grown older trying to hang on to his personal franchise. It was an emotional need to remain a part of the game he loved.

At the end of their careers, a peculiar form of perception widened the gap between Jackie Robinson and Larry Doby on their way to the history books.

Each endured the same humiliations. Each emerged as a superstar. But Jackie started and finished earlier and on top. This was reality, not the movies. The nation's memory of Doby began to shrink. It was as though he was being seen through the wrong end of a set of binoculars, and the illusion shrank both the image and his achievements. The perceived divide between the two grew even wider. It morphed into a conviction that the breaking of the National League's color line by Robinson dwarfed the breaking of the American League's color line by Doby.

After all, once Jackie did it in 1947, it was done. No problem. No story.

Right?

Not really. Not as long as American League owners like Calvin Griffith, without criticism, could explain their moving the American League's Washington Senators, whom he inherited, to Minnesota (after the 1960 season) by proclaiming that he went there because only a small number of "coloreds" lived there and, as he told one group of locals, he was attracted by the presence of "hardworking white people."

Not as long as we were aware of Joe Cronin's response to the cautionary message from the commissioner of baseball, Bowie Kuhn, as told to me by Monte Irvin, the Hall of Famer who delivered it. "It was time to honor Jackie Robinson, and he wanted Cronin out there," Irvin remembered. "Cronin was at a refreshment stand eating a hot dog."

"Can't you see I'm busy?" Cronin told him.

Jackie and Larry faced the same racists, the same Jim Crow cities, the same loneliness, and the same headhunting pitchers. So why the gap when both careers are weighed? You can measure it with simple geography and the cultural divide between Cleveland and New York. Both sets of fans were intensely loyal. Both sets of newspapermen had different attitudes. When Robinson left the Dodgers, New York City's seven local papers lionized him. When Doby left Cleveland after two pennants and a World Series title, one of the columnist's goodbyes was a kind of don't-let-the-door-hit-you-in-the-ass-on-the-way-out tribute.

Now both pioneers had retired. Jackie did well in business. He was the spokesman for Chock full o'Nuts coffee, helped found and was the board chairman of the Freedom National Bank in Harlem. He also worked for Governor Nelson Rockefeller (R-NY) and remained publicly dedicated to civil rights causes.

Doby was also out of baseball, undecided as to what could be next for him. At age thirty-seven, he was still a young man, but in baseball age his legs were ancient. Still, as a baseball lifer, each time he took stock of what skills could be useful in planning his future, his preponderance of knowledge always came up baseball.

He was happy to be with his family, which by then had grown to five children, and Helyn was more than happy for him to be there to shoulder more of the responsibilities with them. But when February rolled around in his first year away from the game, the familiar phrase "pitchers and catchers report this week" generated an emotional itch he couldn't scratch. For the first time, he was a baseball player without a team.

He played a lot of golf. He got to hang out with Joe Taub, his buddy from the old neighborhood, the guy who funded

ADP and for whom he would later work. Eventually, Taub and Doby would put together a Paterson primary school basketball league. He spoke to schoolkids and saw his own childhood hopes reflected in the little faces looking up at him. They were all feel-good things. But they couldn't compete with the moment the roar of a baseball crowd in full crescendo melts into a background murmur . . . when there is no room for it in the mind of the hitter or the pitcher . . . when the core of baseball's classic matchup boils down to "what will he throw, and will I make contact?"

You can't recapture any of it playing catch in the backyard with your kids. And you can't learn to manage until you learn to coach.

Until then, where in the world could an aging baseball lifer find one more at-bat . . . one more fly ball to chase?

Doby never did figure out the answer.

Then, one day, the answer came to him.

But first, there was a domestic debate in the Doby household. The event sticks out even today in the mind of Larry Doby Jr., because it was such a rare thing. "They were in the kitchen, and they were arguing. I knew they were having an argument because I could hear their voices. I was only five years old, but I never heard them raise their voices before or after. They just never did that where we could hear them.

"My dad wanted to invest in a small nightclub and package store. My mom was strongly against it. She said we worked too hard for what we have. He said we need an added income, the way the future looked."

The bar was located at 78 West Market Street. The old Grand Hotel where the Eagles hung out was at 140 West Market. Doby knew the neighborhood. Of more importance, because of the Eagles the neighborhood knew him.

"She was right," Junior said. "At least, she seemed to be. In order to close the deal they had to put down what I guess in those days was a large sum of money. They had set up a college fund for each kid starting before we were even born. They took us to the bank to withdraw it. As kids, we didn't understand. We were excited. We thought each of us was there to get a lot of money."

They opened the bar under the name Larry Doby's Centerfield Lounge. Helyn, the good soldier, regularly helped. When Larry left for Nagoya, Japan, and his next adventure, Helyn's brother, George, the kid Doby used to take to watch him play for Paterson Eastside, and her brother-in-law helped run the place.

It was in Nagoya that the answer to the question Larry Doby couldn't find, when he tried to plan the future, found him.

"As I recall," Doby told Andrew Martin for Medium.com, "two men with an interpreter came into my bar and asked me if I wanted to play in Japan. When I agreed, and the publicity came out, I got a call from Pierre Salinger, President Kennedy's press secretary. You would be representing the president and the United States. He said we had good relationships with the Japanese people, and we could make it even better."

The "we" referred to Don Newcombe, once his Newark Eagles teammate, who as a Brooklyn Dodger won both a Cy Young and an MVP Award and wanted to come out of retirement as well. He had been contacted by the same people before Doby, had agreed, and then called his old teammate to give him a heads-up that they were coming to see him.

They signed with the Chunichi Dragons, who were based in Nagoya, a city about two hundred miles from Tokyo. Doby would play first and the outfield and bat third; Newcombe, one of the best hitting pitchers in the history of the game, would play left field and bat fourth. Doby was thirty-eight, Newcombe thirty-six.

Obviously, at those ages, they were shadows of what they had once been. Doby had not played in a game for two years, and it took a laborious effort for him to get in shape. But the professionalism they brought with them made a powerful impact. When they joined the team, the Dragons were in last place, dispirited and not very good.

The two were stepping into a world that bore little resemblance to the one they had recently left. This was Japan's version of their national game. The atmosphere was more college football than Major League Baseball. Cheerleaders danced on top of the dugouts. Fans sang and chanted their team's songs. Each team was owned by industrialists who often added their corporate name to their team's colloquial nicknames.

Newcombe brought his family and rented a house. Doby lived in a modern hotel. But on the road, they stayed with the team in Japanese accommodations, eating and sitting on the floor. Both men became autograph targets and local heroes.

They did not tear up Japanese pitchers. But they did hit enough home runs to live up to Nagoya fans' thirst for the kind of power Japanese-born players rarely displayed, and they brought a unique American optimism to the park each day. They changed the Dragons from a disheartened team waiting for the season to end into a group that suddenly found fun in what they did. Doby, a natural teacher, improved the team's baseball knowledge.

Together they triggered the exact attitude Chunichi needed to rise from last place to third, finishing 10 games over .500.

Despite the undeniable fact that age had robbed them of many of their skills, both Newcombe and Doby were pleased with their performances and the respect shown them by the fans, whether in restaurants, movie theaters, or out taking a walk. They also discovered that they had an unexpected mentor.

His name was Wally Yonamine, and they had come to realize that while both men had shared loneliness, isolation, and racist scorn as Black men breaking a century-long color line after they left the Eagles, Yonamine had survived a similar kind of taboo in total silence.

Yonamine was two years younger than Doby, born on the island of Maui, the son of a Japanese father and an Okinawan mother. At the end of World War II, he joined the Tokyo Giants and immediately was the most hated player in all of Japan—a yellow-skinned American who couldn't speak Japanese, treading where no American player had dared to, with the war still fresh in the minds of the Japanese. To them, because of his skin color and his American citizenship, he was the worst *gaijin* (foreigner) of all.

Yonamine was a rowdy, base-stealing, hard-sliding, superb hitting outfielder who brought a kind of game to Japan that the country didn't even know existed. Until they learned from him how baseball was really played, they had been all polite bows and nobody challenging the umpire. Yonamine had a thirty-eight-year career there as a player, manager, and consultant. Incredibly, the same people who booed him all year voted him to their All-Star Game in a landslide. As a teammate, he served as interpreter for the two *gaijins* and as a friend.

I knew Yonamine when I was serving on the Pacific Stars and Stripes newspaper organization after the Korean armistice. He told me about the way it was for him. "Back then, most of the outfielders threw sidearm," he remembered. "When I hit what should have been a single, I just kept running."

For Doby, Yonamine's friendship became a personal inspiration. Yonamine confided to him that he too eventually wanted to become a manager. They both made it. More remarkably, Doby would become an American Hall of Famer and Yonamine would be the first foreigner inducted into the Japanese Baseball Hall of Fame.

There was nothing Zen-like about Doby's return from Asia. Financially, the trip was a reasonable success. The Dragons paid him thirty grand and covered all his living expenses. Artistically, it was far from a return to glory, as evidenced by the fact that they did not invite him back, which was a disappointment, as he felt that the disparity in baseball talent between here and Japan might have given him a more successful second season. Certainly, the Nagoya fans appreciated him. One personal bright spot he took away was in the strong relationship he developed with the younger players who were eager to learn from him. That and Yonamine's determination to one day manage matched Doby's own goals. Meanwhile, he was reasonably happy running the bar with Helyn's help. Unlike for most of his baseball career, he didn't have to impress anyone.

But in 1965, the business could not be saved. The neighborhood did not support it. He sold it at a net loss of $40,000. It was typical of what became their fifty-five-year marriage that Helyn, who had opposed the purchase, never said, "I told you so."

You might take the boy out of baseball, but not the man. In recurring interviews, Doby always made his feelings known about the fact that not a single Black person was a manager or holding a significant front-office job. His words resonated because they were true. A new wind was blowing across America, and something significant was carrying along with it. At first it seemed to be beyond the ken of baseball. It was triggered by Dr. Martin Luther King Jr. . . . by the riots that began in Newark and Detroit . . . by the first American troops sent to Vietnam. For some time, the question "Can he hit the curve?" had become more relevant than "What's the color of his skin?"

Meanwhile, Doby worked in the Essex County prosecutor's office and even mediated a serious racial dispute among students at Barringer High School. Adults of a certain age who were students at the time clearly remember the lecture he gave them.

Doby, Jackie Robinson, and two-time MVP Frank Robinson would not stay silent. The new group of Black players supported their assertions. The players and the fans began to understand social change. As Doby told his biographer Joe Moore, "My question is that if the owners looked at it from a positive standpoint, why is it Black coaches never get the chance to coach at third? Why do they only coach at first?" The answer, of course, is that the third-base coach has more responsibilities, and they are the ones who most often become managers.

Baseball has always been strangled in a self-serving web of what jurists call "the social lag"—the web cast between what we want and need and the executives who are slow to do something about it. The growing talk about the racial gaps between players and managers did not go unnoticed by then commissioner William Eckert, which explains his blessing to a 1968 private dinner date at the sports-oriented Toots Shor's watering hole in Manhattan, involving Doby, Monte Irvin, and Kuhn's assistant John McHale, who was about to become the president of the expansion Montreal Expos.

The way Doby relayed it to me was that McHale told them he had two jobs. "The first was executive assistant to the commissioner, which Monte wanted," Doby said, "and the other was as a scout in the Expos organization. That was fine with me because I wanted to be where the action was again."

The Expos job was not exactly as advertised. He spent the first season as a roving minor-league scout. It wasn't what Doby had signed on for, but when manager Gene Mauch saw what Doby had achieved with the young prospects during a single season, he acted immediately—bringing him up to the big team as the Expos' new hitting coach.

Doby related to the young Black players, for obvious reasons, and he had the knowledge and approach to get the attention of the young whites as well.

As a case in point, although Larry Jr. could not recall the name, he told me of a young outfielder from Georgia, whose slow, Southern drawl sounded as though it were drowning in a bucket of grits. "Junior," the player said, "without your pappy I ain't shit." That year, for the first time in his minor-league career, he hit 15 home runs.

After high praise from Mauch, Doby returned to the Indians as a coach in 1974, and was assigned to the first-base coaching box. When manager Ken Aspromonte was fired, all of Cleveland—including several players—expected Doby to be named the first

Black manager. Instead, another Black star, Frank Robinson, got the job. Doby went back to Montreal and rejoined the coaching staff, first as a minor-league batting consultant and then as the big team's batting coach. Meanwhile, he added to his résumé by managing winter-league teams in Venezuela.

The network of whisperers had their own explanation as to why baseball didn't want Doby as a manager or a front-office executive. His supporters had their own rebuttals. Frank Robinson pulled no punches when he was asked if Doby was on the outside looking in: "Larry gave his all to this game. Is intelligent. He could make a meaningful contribution in the front office. But Larry has a characteristic in common with me. He is outspoken. They don't want a Negro like that."

As Exhibit One, there was this, told by Doby to the *Chicago Tribune* in 1987, in all candor: "It's still not the all-American game because all Americans cannot work in baseball in most positions. How can they keep saying it is hot dogs and apple pie and motherhood and all that? I don't know."

Some of the media were defensive about that. All of the owners were more defensive about that—all except one. Bill Veeck, lifelong friend to Larry, godfather to Larry Jr., and one of the few men in baseball with both conscience and caring. Now he was back, as the new owner of the Chicago White Sox. He later brought Doby over as a coach.

But in early July, he was in the middle of a non-baseball morality play.

For traveling ballplayers, the old time-killer used to be lobby-sitting, but after Doby's playing career was over, lobbies had been "replaced" by watching TV soap operas.

The White Sox had a night game. Alone in his room that morning, he sat on his bed staring at the television set, trying to follow an episode more challenging than the signals for a double steal. *Trish had this baby. And Michael knew he was the father.* Doby leaned forward. *Would Michael do the honorable thing: marry her even though he loved someone else?*

And that's when the phone rang. Bill Veeck, on the other end, said he would appreciate it if Doby would come down to his suite. Since Mr. Doby was in Minnesota for a game against the Twins and since Mr. Veeck signed his paycheck, Doby sighed, left the TV on, and closed the door behind him, leaving Michael to screw it up on his own.

Twenty minutes later, Larry Doby was no longer watching a soap opera. He was starring in one.

"Hello, Lawrence," Veeck said.

"Hello, William," Larry said.

"How would you like to manage my ballclub?"

"Well, yeah. I guess so."

"Good," Veeck replied. "I already have taken the liberty of calling a press conference."

So this is how the dream came to Larry Doby, though it was not exactly a gift. The team he was given was halfway through the 1978 season held a record of 34–40. It was also a bittersweet moment, because the man he replaced was his old friend and former teammate Bob Lemon. Coming off the previous season in which the team went 90–72, the Sox still had a slight chance, though it depended more on whether the real contenders would suddenly move backward, even if he produced a miracle, which with this team he could not. He would have been better served if he were further behind and could have been judged solely upon the improvement he could make. But it didn't work like that. He was a local favorite hired to take some of the heat off management.

The Sox went 37–50 with their new skipper at the helm, finishing fifth, and Doby was not given a second chance.

Instead, based on their long friendship, Veeck rehired him as the team's batting coach. A year later, he resigned. He never managed again. But Doby and baseball were not even close to done with each other.

CHAPTER 11

JACKIE'S LAST STAND, LARRY'S NEW LIFE

Jackie Robinson died on October 24, 1972. Roughly a week earlier, he stood on the field at Cincinnati's Riverfront Stadium before the second game of the 1972 World Series. Next to him were Larry Doby, who broke the American League color line, and Joe Black, a former Brooklyn teammate. The pregame silence was broken by a thunderous greeting from the crowd of 53,224 when they saw him. When baseball commissioner Bowie Kuhn first invited him to the ceremony to honor the twenty-fifth anniversary of his breaking baseball's color line, Robinson had refused to attend.

He told columnist Ron Rapoport of the *Los Angeles Times*, "Baseball and Jackie Robinson haven't had much to say to each other."

Robinson added, "I told Dodgers president Peter O'Malley I am disturbed at the way baseball treats its Black players after their playing days are through. It's hard to look at a sport which Black athletes have virtually saved and when a managerial job opens they give it to a guy who has failed in other areas because he is white."

Kuhn, with crucial help from his administrative assistant, Hall of Famer Monte Irvin, explained the planning that his office had begun to remedy the lack of Black managers and front-office personnel. Robinson said he would attend. Part of his rationale was the notion that he would speak his mind to a massive television audience.

Jackie being Jackie, that's exactly why he changed his mind and said what he said. The presence of Doby and Black at his side served to certify a new wake-up call for baseball. Jackie knew that Doby wanted to manage and that Black had been rejected for several front-office jobs. His words were a personal call to arms that eventually strengthened Kuhn's plan to wipe out yet another color line. In effect, they formed a second Robinson legacy falling on the right ears, a kind of public-relations factor that made it easier to sign Doby as a manager than it had been to sign him as a player.

At that point in his life, daily pain was Jackie's enemy. Though just fifty-three years old, his body had been ravaged by advanced diabetes. He was blind in one eye and needed assistance to walk. His hair was snowy-white. But he knew his words still carried weight. And he knew that of all possible venues, this one was special for him. As a rookie he had received two verifiable death threats when he played his first game in Cincinnati a quarter a century earlier. This was the city where his captain, Pee Wee Reese, raised in Louisville, Kentucky, draped an arm over Jackie's shoulder and laughed at the bigots.

When Jackie spoke, he obviously knew the end was near. But you could not hear it in the timbre of his voice. He was telling the world what he believed from the start. The mission hadn't changed. For him, the job couldn't end short of its goal. His message was clear. It trumpeted a belief from which he never wavered:

"I was really just a spoke in the wheel of the success that we had some twenty-five years ago. . . . I'm extremely proud and pleased to be here this afternoon, but must admit I'm gonna be tremendously more pleased and more proud when I look at that third-base coaching line one day and see a Black face managing in baseball."

Those words were delivered with such intensity they seemed to stop the calendar. In that moment, the vision was no longer blurred, the legs no longer weak, the hair no longer white. The voice was firm because he knew he was delivering a message whose time should have come decades earlier. On that day, he was the messenger. Larry Doby, at his side, would be the living embodiment of Robinson's call to arms. It is well worth noting that on that day they were both still fighting for the same goals. Sadly, also on that day, seeing Jackie and Larry together, a lot of folks still failed to understand their personal relationship.

For starters, when Jackie broke the color line in April 1947 and Doby broke the American League line in July, it was only natural that Jackie would get all the attention. By the end of that season, Jackie was a confirmed superstar on a team that welcomed him with open arms while Larry barely received playing time from a mostly cold locker room. From that simple chronological fact, a misguided belief grew that the two were performing in two different universes.

Different? Not very much when Jackie was still in Montreal and Syracuse players threw a black cat on the field and yelled, "Hey, here's your cousin!"

And not when Tom Yawkey, a millionaire racist who owned the Boston Red Sox, said, "Anyone who claims I am a racist should look at my farm down South, where I hire a lot of Negroes." Not when Tom Yawkey was the very last owner in all of baseball—in 1959—to have a Black player on their big-league roster.

The truth is that Jackie and Larry spoke on the telephone constantly that first year about the shared burden thrust upon them and how to possibly deal with it. The silent agreement between them was that they would manage it, fight it through to the end, whatever the final result would be and, most of all, remember not to lose their cool. For this last, with mutual resolve. It wasn't easy, but thanks to those late-night telephone calls, they were, along with their wives, their own best support system.

Actually, despite dealing with the race problem, the two men were far from the same. They were, however, quite similar. "If anyone believes that Larry was jealous of all the attention Jackie received while Larry got little credit, then they don't know Larry Doby," his Cleveland teammate Al Rosen once said. Jackie's thoughts were often fired by a justifiable hair-trigger temper once he was established. Conversely, Larry would internalize the same anger, but when he finally released it there was no doubt where he stood. I knew Larry a long, long time, and the measure of respect he felt for Robinson could be weighed by a simple fact.

Every single time he mentioned his co-pioneer to me, in any conversation, he never called him Jackie, never called him Robinson. It was always "Mr. Robinson." I also heard him say it that way every time he was interviewed. If there were three other people in his answer, he would generally use their last name in the same sentence when he invariably referred to Jackie as Mr.

Robinson. To me, that was a signal about his early upbringing in Camden, South Carolina. You can take the boy out of South Carolina, but not South Carolina out of the man. I heard Larry refer to very few people as "Mister." They were people for whom he had the utmost respect. He was a pallbearer at Jackie's funeral. And Rachel Robinson was there in the little church in Montclair, New Jersey, when they laid Larry to rest.

One side note here about Robinson. His first roommate in his rookie season was a Black pitcher purchased from the all-Black Memphis Red Sox. His name was Dan Bankhead and, over the course of three seasons (1947, 1950–1951) in which he shuttled between Montreal and Brooklyn, he appeared in 52 games and posted a meager but winning history. In 1953, he was back in Montreal and Brooklyn was in the World Series.

He walked into the Dodgers office in Brooklyn and asked for a complimentary World Series ticket.

"Screw him," a middle-echelon Dodgers official said. "He should have saved his money."

Bankhead's highest salary with the Dodgers was $7,500. He was the first Black man to pitch in a World Series. Like Robinson, he could not live in the players' hotels or sleep where they slept. It was Branch Rickey himself who scouted and signed Bankhead. A hard-to-get lower-stand ticket for Game Two had a box-office value of $7.00. Maybe the Dodgers should have given up the seven bucks using the money he didn't pay the Kansas City Monarchs to sign Jackie.

Larry's rebuttal to the jealousy idea was simple. "I was never bitter," as he said, "because I believe in the man upstairs. I continue to do my best. If I were ever bitter, I was only hurting me. I prefer to remember Bill Veeck and Mike Hegan and Joe

Gordon, the good guys. There is no point even talking about the others."

Robinson and Doby are forever linked in history, just as you can't say "Ali" without thinking "Frazier." Today, if you know anything about baseball, or the civil rights struggle, or the history of the game America invented, you can't say "Robinson" without thinking "Doby." That's why I took what happened on a cold, rainy night in 1985 before a Cardinals-Dodgers playoff game as an affront to the two of them. Vince Coleman of the Cardinals was on the field right after batting practice, and I asked him if he knew that the anniversary of Robinson's death was coming up and what it meant to him.

"What the fuck I care?" he said. "He never put any bread and butter on my table." Apparently he was absent the day his high school history class discussed it.

As Coleman turned away, the drizzle threatened to become serious rain. In that exact moment, the grounds crew started to cover the field. Busch Stadium had an automatic mechanical tarp. Once they hit the switch, there was no turning back. While Coleman turned, it caught his ankle. Wrapped in the tarp, he was a prisoner of whatever gods rule baseball. It chipped a bone in his leg.

I remember turning to our beat writer, Rich Chere, as the tarp tightened around Coleman's leg, and telling him, "Let that be a lesson to you. God is a baseball fan."

If I had been talking to Coleman about Doby, I am sure I would have gotten the same response. Coleman was part of a group that believed they would been special without Larry or Jackie, but I question whether they would have paid the same price. Paving the way. Coleman proved that after he signed with the Mets and wound up throwing fireworks at some fans in the Dodger Stadium parking lot after a game.

After Jackie was gone, Larry still wanted to be the first Black manager. He almost did it when he became the Indians' first-base coach. When Frank Robinson got the job and his place in history as the first Black manager, Doby soldiered on. When Veeck later bought the White Sox and named him the manager, Doby's reaction echoed the challenge voiced by Jackie that day in Cincinnati. He was reminded that after the earlier close call, he was now fifty-three years old. In Brooklyn, it had been Jackie Robinson and the Dodgers against the world. . . . but in Cleveland, it had been Larry Doby and a handful of volunteers against the universe.

"Why did it take this long? You tell me," Doby once said. "I don't mean to sound prejudiced, but you can look at the system and see that when I was named, and Frank Robinson was gone, there was no Black manager but me in the major leagues."

After Veeck replaced Doby as the White Sox' interim manager, he kept him on for a season as the batting coach and then moved on. Doby never knew the exact reason Veeck fired him.

Mike Veeck once said that his father told Larry, "That's a conversation we don't need to have. If we do, we'll both end up crying before it's over."

The Sox were headed nowhere under Bob Lemon primarily because they were not particularly good, even though they had won 90 games the previous season, raising Veeck's expectations. Showman that Veeck always was, I suspected Doby was hired in the hope that a popular Black manager could stimulate attendance from the heavily Black South Side of the city. But that kind of impact doesn't happen if you don't win games. And they didn't. Mediocre as the talent was, Mandrake the Magician could not have made them better.

Doby had no way of knowing how well he had managed. He just didn't have enough time. When he was out of baseball, he told Bob Harding from my newspaper, "I am still working in athletics [community relations director for the NBA's New Jersey Nets], but as you can see the athletes are a lot taller. But, yes, I would go back to baseball if a manager's job was offered. Managing a baseball team has a lot of challenges and I am a man who has to have a challenge in his life. Actually, I can't evaluate how much of an impact I had as a manager because I only had half a season. And when I took over, we were too far back."

After he was out as manager of the White Sox, he was ignored by many in the game to which he gave so much. Out of sight became out of mind for the memories he should have generated. For far too long he was relegated to a position in the collective minds of the nation that didn't equate to an enduring shelf life and wasn't worth much. He had integrated the entire American League, but the feeling was, "Well, wasn't Jackie Robinson number one? Didn't Jackie end the color line?" And as good a player as Doby was, "not being number one" was and is a typical American slight. In America, number two is just a number.

The question became: "What is being second worth?"

For me, the best analysis of that dilemma I ever heard came from the late Nick Buoniconti, the Hall of Fame linebacker for the (then) Boston Patriots and Miami Dolphins. His Dolphins were undefeated in 1972 and headed for the Super Bowl the following week. I sat down with him after their last practice before they flew to California for the big game.

"We gotta win this game," he said, "or nothing we have done this entire season will mean anything. Nobody will remember us."

"That's ridiculous. Do you realize how many teams won't even be there?"

"Yeah, so who will remember who finished last?" he replied. "Nobody. But everybody will know who lost the Super Bowl game. Being number two gets us absolutely nothing."

He was right. Running the second four-minute mile meant nothing. Who talks about the second man on the moon? And for a long time, baseball let Larry Doby melt away into a classic trivia question: Who was the second standard-bearer of integration?

Not that it bothered him. With apologies to General Douglas MacArthur, who quoted an old barracks song about his retirement, "Old soldiers never die, they just fade away." Once Larry was out of baseball, his role in history faded like that metaphorical old soldier.

According to baseball, Doby had run his race. It was time for him to fade away. Nobody made a job offer. He was pondering his future during a discussion with Joe Taub, his old neighborhood buddy and the majority owner of the then-New Jersey Nets, asked him, "Listen, why don't you just come home and work for me?" It made sense. So he did.

In 1979, Taub named him the team's community relations director. Basketball was hardly alien territory for Doby. At Paterson Eastside High School, he had been an all-state basketball player, earning a scholarship from nationally ranked LIU. In his first baseball offseason, he played professionally for the

Paterson Crescents of the American Basketball League. He was the first Black to do so.

The renewal of the Taub-Doby friendship took some of the sting out of the disappointments that marked the end of his career. He was home, and probably for the first time since his free and easy days with the Newark Eagles, there were no pressures and nothing to prove. Of course, he wanted and missed the spot he deserved in the Baseball Hall of Fame, but he never believed he would be given it in the first place—just as he believed he would never get a second chance to manage. And Doby being Doby, he never focused on the things he didn't have. Instead, for the first time he could sit back, relax and enjoy his new life.

He understood the new challenge with Taub and the Nets, and coupled with their shared memories of the old neighborhood, it made for a comfortable relationship. Then there was golf with his pal and neighbor Yogi Berra, the first American League opponent to welcome him to baseball and his co-conspirator when they hid out at the American Legion post in Montclair any time either wife had a chore that needed to be done. There was the new challenge with the Nets and his role in a new job that was not clearly defined. He ran the Taub-Doby elementary school basketball league. He was a liaison between the Nets' PR people and the media. He was readily available as the franchise's goodwill ambassador for charity programs. And with the team starved for respectability, the beat writers always got something from Larry.

He was also unofficially in charge of the team's gifted but erratic star, Micheal "Sugar Ray" Richardson, a task I am sure he never talked about to me . . . not to his family . . . and I suspect not to anybody. He had to make sure Sugar got to work on time, make sure he could continue guiding him toward maturity. Sugar had a drug problem, but Doby kept him as close to straight as he could. Sugar eventually did straighten out, played overseas, and got a coaching job. I'm sure Doby's caring and input had a lot to do with that turnaround.

Unless you were his coach, you had to smile when you heard Richardson's name and remembered that he gave us an immortal quote: "The ship be sinking."

Doby's impact on the Nets front office was considerable. "I remember the first day he came to work," said Mitch Kaufman, a member of the Nets' video staff. "He wore a brown pinstripe suit with a matching pocket square. The guy you need to talk to about his contribution is Howard Freeman, our promotions guy. They worked together."

"They say people outside of New Jersey forgot him," Freeman put in. "Perhaps, but in Jersey everybody knew him. I ran the promotions department, and he was my backstage pass. He opened tons of doors for us. He was a dream co-worker.

"One day, Joe Taub booked a softball game, our front office against the ADP front office, another company he had founded.

"'You gotta play for the Nets,'" Joe told Doby.

"'But Joe, I—"

"'Don't "but Joe" me—you're playing.'"

"We played on some field in Nutley, New Jersey," recalled Lou Terminello, the sales director. "And Doby put on a clinic in batting practice: five line drives down the left-field line . . . five line drives down the right-field line . . . and five monsters to direct center. He was so close to Paterson after all those years that when they held a memorial dinner for [legendary comedian] Lou

Costello, we went. You would have thought they were honoring Larry. Everybody wanted to shake his hand."

In December of his first year in retirement, Larry was asked to join the city of Paterson's recreation department. But still, discussions of the early years and what happened back then were not on the table for Larry Jr.

"It reminds me," Junior said, "of the guys who served in a war. When they came home, they didn't talk about it. I always felt he didn't want his pain to shape my view of the game. He thought that part was something only for those who shared it. Mr. Irvin visited with us. Mr. Newcombe was always on the phone. What I learned about my dad's struggles I learned by eavesdropping when they were talking."

One thing I learned during those years was that those among the Cleveland writers who labeled him as aloof, bitter, self-absorbed, and racist might have been experts in the infield fly rule and what constitutes a ground-rule double at Municipal Stadium, but never tried to understand who Larry Doby really was and what shaped him as a man. Hell, based on what they wrote (elsewhere in this book), when he played in Cleveland they didn't have a clue about the impact of the imposed Jim Crow lifestyle under which the first Black man in the American League was forced to live. I doubt if any of them gave a thought as to why he was a member of a team with whom he could neither eat nor share a hotel. Whether overt or subliminal, I believe it was a clear case of being easier to go along to get along.

So why? Why was it so hard to overlook the notion that death threats matter or that dehumanizing does not breed teamwork?

It could have been a subliminal fear. I doubt any of them had a reason to even know anyone who was Black. It could have been ignorance. It could have been a sense of uneasiness about challenging what had been the norm for so long in that era. It could have been the honest lack of wanting a teammate to fail so he wouldn't be a teammate.

When I retired as an active member of the Baseball Writers' Association of America, my membership card was actually number three out of perhaps a couple hundred of us. One undeniable fact never changed between then and now. Trust is an essential that leads to truth between writer and athlete. Trust is two-sided. A couple of the major writers and shapers of opinion in Cleveland expected Larry to give without receiving it from them.

But more than two decades later, respect (combined with good intentions and baseball's guilt) finally got to shine an unexpected light on a career so many had forgotten. For many, it wasn't just a wake-up call. It was an education.

CHAPTER 12

THE FAMILY TIES AND A FIELD OF HIS OWN

For as long as Mike Veeck can remember, they were two families indivisible—the Veecks and the Dobys—whose patriarchs taught him to laugh at the cowardice of racism, rush to embrace the joys of life, and never forget where they came from and who they were. To best explain the way in which the two families shared the burdens and the triumphs of what the two men had experienced, you have to understand that, in tandem, these men did more than integrate the American League; more than change the course of America's social history; more than look the worst of America in the eye and confront it until, little by little, it moved toward being the best.

"I can't remember when I first noticed Larry," Mike told me. "But he was always with me in some way. First, I knew him as a picture on a baseball card. Then I grew older and began to know him as a person. We both know the kind of man he was. He had a presence, and it always dealt with the truth. He was the faith of the civil rights movement. . . . He was faith itself . . . faith in tomorrow. Over the years I have owned a number of minor- and iindependent league ballclubs, and one year I brought all the front offices together for a meeting. And I brought Larry, too, and asked him to speak to them.

"He walked into the room. There must have been forty people. He looked them directly in the eye, and then he took them on a journey they couldn't possibly have imagined. . . . The terrible and sure as hell separate Black rooming houses without air conditioning . . . the cabs that would not pick him up and made him walk back to sit alone in his room while a cheap fan tried to blow cold air off a cake of ice . . . the threats . . . the pain and the constant loneliness.

"And he told us something about bringing more Black fans to baseball. Later, when he was hired by the American League office, he tried to tell them the same thing. He said what kept the poor Blacks away was more than the price of a ticket. He said to negotiate a low-price ticket that also included a hot dog and a soda at a price they could afford."

There is this incredible need to do the right thing, and this joy in doing it, that always united these two families. It is the legacy of shared pain that began when Bill Veeck told the American League to go to hell by signing Doby and launched him on a journey that made Mike and Larry the two most isolated people in baseball.

"I remember our last trip to Cooperstown," said Mike Veeck, "and watching him and Helyn; my mother, Mary Francis; his daughters laughing; and the man himself. In a mocha-brown pinstripe suit, surrounded by 'his girls,' remembering only the good times, and Henry Aaron and Stan Musial coming over to thank him for what he did, which is what should have happened."

With what the two families experienced, it is no surprise that values and memories were passed down to the next generations. Like his father, Mike Veeck became a baseball man. Every team he ever owned or ran bore evidence of the battles his father and Larry fought and won—murals of Larry, displays of his uniform. And then there was the ritual.

The first time they did it, he was the promotions guy for the Tampa Bay Devil Rays. It began with Mike's little girl, Rebecca, holding a baseball just outside the stadium in St. Petersburg, Florida, on Opening Day 1999. She passed it to Helyn Doby next to her, who in turn passed it to Bill Veeck's widow, Mary Francis, who passed it down the line more than a mile through the city, through the poorest of neighborhoods and back to Bill Veeck's granddaughter, who ran inside the park and presented it to Larry Doby, who then threw out the ceremonial first pitch.

A lot of fans and more players on the field than you might think learned a lot about Lawrence Eugene Doby that day. In all, we honored Doby in various ways in fifteen baseball parks. And to complete their eternal circle, Bill Veeck was Larry Jr.'s honorary godfather.

The Yogi Berra Museum and Learning Center sits on Yogi Berra Drive, a tree-lined street on the Little Falls side of the Montclair State University campus in New Jersey. It was built as Montclair's gift to its most recognizable citizen, not far from the stadium that bears his name. It is a measure of Yogi's respect that inside the building, one room is dedicated to Doby and filled with his memorabilia.

Berra was the first American Leaguer to acknowledge his presence on the other side of the league's color line. They were friends ever since Doby came to bat against the Yankees for the first time. As he dug in, Yogi asked, "How is your family doin'?" The second time Doby dug in, Yogi asked again: "How is the family doin'?"

"The same as when you asked me in the first inning," Doby responded. Then he turned to the umpire and said, "Please tell him to shut up and let me hit."

"Oh, OK. I talk to everyone."

That was the start of a beautiful friendship, one that gave meaning to the time they enjoyed after both left the game. Between Yogi and Joe Taub, Larry stayed busy. And slowly, without fanfare, people were noticing. Doby was inducted into the Cleveland Indians Hall of Fame in 1963; in 1973, the State of South Carolina Hall of Fame inducted him.

Jackie Robinson was deservedly inducted into the National Baseball Hall Fame in 1962. There were no complaints—nor should there have been. From his debut forward, he was truly one of the most dynamic stars of the game. But the frustrating road that led Larry Doby to that same place didn't come until 1998—fifty-one years from the day he broke the American League color line in 1947.

What had begun as a separate and unequal rookie season morphed to the point where he became an elder statesman in the Cleveland locker room, matching his brilliant All-Star performances on the field. In 1994, the Cleveland Indians retired his uniform No. 14. A street near Progressive Field, the team's home park, was renamed Larry Doby Way in 2012. The franchise built a statue in his honor in 2015 and placed it in front of an entrance to the stadium. But no matter the honors, he was still always locked in Jackie's shadow. His triumphs always seemed a little less than the recognition of Jackie as the first.

Major League Baseball retired Robinson's No. 42 forever in both leagues in 1997. The American League did nothing for Larry's No. 14.

I still remember that 1997 night at Shea Stadium in New York when Jackie's No. 42 was worn by all the players and then formally enshrined. It was billed as a tribute to Robinson, and a tribute to what Rachel Robinson had endured, but something about the evening bothered me. I figured it out when I saw the starting lineups on the big scoreboard. Alongside the lineups was a message that a beer company was proud to present them.

When you consider what Jackie (and Larry) endured, that bit of business as usual struck me as a thank-you to a mugger for finally not hitting you anymore.

On July 5, 2023, the renamed Cleveland Guardians celebrated the 76th anniversary of Doby's debut in the majors. Before ceremonies began, Guardians manager Terry Fracona suddenly raced into the dugout, picked up a silver pen, took off his cap, and printed a large "14" on the crown.

"I had not planned that," Francona told reporters afterward. "I looked over to where Doby's family was, and I saw Larry Doby Jr. Most people don't know that when my dad [Tito] was a player, he was traded twice for Larry Doby. So, in a way, my family was part of his career.

"Junior's father couldn't sleep in any hotel where white players slept," Francona added. "He couldn't eat in any restaurant where the white players ate. Maybe it's not much of a statement, but in this town it will help a lot of folks never to forget."

To reinforce that idea, the team front office announced that night it had made a request to MLB: Make sure the Guardians always play at home on the anniversary date, July 5, of Doby's historic debut.

But there were people in Paterson who never forgot the young man who matriculated at Eastside High School and became—and is still recognized as—the greatest athlete in the school's history. For them, there was the state football championship in which he played a major role. Along with the well-above-.400 batting averages that were countywide news, and his leadership qualities on the basketball court. There was his spectacular major-league career with the Indians and, most of all, the shattering of the American League color line. All of which induced a former mayor to tell the Paterson electorate, "He gave Paterson far more than Paterson gave him."

In 1998, the Battle of Cooperstown was won by the Doby advocates, and we will explain in a subsequent chapter how that happened. But for Paterson, it still wasn't enough. The city's movers and shakers wanted something that linked him forever with Paterson. Nobody suggested they bronze his bat—they wanted to bronze all of him. They wanted to bestow on him even more of a singular honor that reflected civic pride.

It came together on the same swatch of land he once owned each time he showed up in an Eastside High School uniform, and in the steamy Paterson summer when school was out and the uniform shirt had the name "Smart Set" across it. The choice was prophetic. No matter what uniform he wore between the ages of seventeen and twenty, with a bat in his hands he absolutely owned that slice of Eastside Park.

So they gave him that as well.

The statue weighs six hundred pounds and stands, like Doby himself, six feet and one half inch tall. It echoes his signature moment: the way he held the bat ear-high before he dropped it down and then straight up, power lodged within his body; and it all melts into a short stride that was his punctuation mark when bat hit ball and it was not a question of if but how far.

When he was asked for his reaction, he responded with the best of memories that flooded his mind. "It's important to go back to where it all began. The old neighborhood . . . the guys sitting on the front steps on summer nights just talking sports . . . the cowboy movies at the Majestic. And this field. I really loved this field."

It is the gift of the city to the next generation, a bookmark for the young players who will follow, a place where its history will whisper in its ears: "He is forever ours. You are forever ours. Learn from him. Learn how he lived. Learn where you can go, but most of all never forget where you came from. Remember him and the field that bears his name. But now Doby's legacy."

Now the kids who play on Larry Doby Field are heavily Hispanic, a relatively new addition to the old neighborhood with the same lessons to be learned. The land doesn't change. We borrow it just as Larry Doby once borrowed this land, and we use it or abuse it. But it never belongs to us. Yes, the dirt infield is long gone, replaced by suitable grass. When the field was originally laid out, home plate faced the wrong way and the men who played on it were part of the heart and soul of Paterson. That was when a trip across the Hudson to Yankee Stadium, with the necessary price of a ticket, was less accessible than a visit to Merlin's Grotto.

Paterson had its own baseball heroes back then—the Paterson Silk Sox, the Glen Rock Athletic Association, the Uncle Sams, the Smart Set, and a semipro game every day when two thousand people were crammed sardine-tight into wooden bleachers and their sponsors passed the hat during the seventh-inning stretch. The roots sprouted on this field for Larry Doby, the very roots that were strong enough to sustain and carry him to a hard-rock long-climb journey all the way to Cooperstown and the National Baseball Hall of Fame.

THE STATUE
Unveiled: 1/6/2002
Sculptor: Phil Sgobba
Material: Bronze
Inscription (s):

Plaque: LAWRENCE EUGENE DOBY. "LARRY." Born Camden, South Carolina, December 13, 1923; . . . Eastside High School, Paterson, 1938–1942; . . . Lettered in Football, Basketball, Baseball, and Track; . . . All-State in Football, Basketball, and Baseball; . . . Attended L.I. University; . . . Negro League, 1942, 1946-1947; . . . U.S. Navy, 1943-1946; . . . American League, 1947–1959; . . . First African American Player in the American League; . . . First African American to hit a home run in the World Series; . . . American League All-Star, 1949–1955; . . . Led the League in Home Runs in 1952; . . .

> Led the League in Home Runs and RBIs in 1954; . . . Manager of the Chicago White Sox, 1978; . . . Baseball Hall of Fame, 1998; . . . Eastside High School Hall of Fame, 1999.

The driving force in creating the statue was Taub, often Doby's lunch companion at the original Harold's New York Deli, not far from the Meadowlands Sports Complex in Jersey. Taub was a part owner and Doby did not like to take doggy bags home. Taub was forceful ("Larry, take pastrami, Helyn will love it. Harold, make him a nice box"). He was so genuine and insistent he sounded like a carnival barker auditioning to carry a sandwich board. It was their regular post-baseball ritual.

The Eastside Park statue was the first of three to honor Doby. The second one stands outside the Guardians' home ballpark, Progressive Field, as a daily reminder that the man passed their way, won a rare Cleveland World Series, integrated the American League, and is a Hall of Famer. The third stands in front of a simple wood-frame building dedicated to local Afro-American history in his birthplace of Camden, South Carolina. As a tribute to a successful local hero, this modest museum contains memorabilia documenting his career.

I cannot help when I think of the field they named after him about the incredible and cruel and lonely times he told me about. How did he handle it? Other than Jackie, who could? And Jackie did not have it easy, but I believe Larry had even fewer allies and far less help. As I write this, there is a picture of Larry on the wall in my direct line of vision. It could have been the model for the Paterson Eastside Park statue. The bat is cocked and loaded and his face is all business. Yes, he signed his name on it and called me "friend." But there is another legend printed in yellow at the top:

"I cannot change yesterday. I can only make the most of today, and look with hope toward tomorrow."

That last line, those indelible words, are also etched on the plaque at Larry Doby Field.

That was really the essence of Lawrence Eugene Doby.

CHAPTER 13
UNKNOWN SOLDIER NO MORE

Larry Doby knew he probably would never manage again. When he led the White Sox for 87 games, he learned a basic axiom that was never wrong. Without good players, managers have no measuring stick to judge their own work.

But good players could make you a great manager. He traveled through every high and low that comprise a baseball lifer's experience. During the twilight days of his career, he entered a new stage of self-discovery. As a manager, he didn't have enough time to find out. But as a hitting coach, he discovered that he had both the knowledge to give and the need to give it.

The skin color of a prospect didn't matter. If necessary, he could communicate effectively with a young player from the "hood," the suburbs, or Latin America with equal facility. "I don't believe it matters if you really want to communicate," he once told me. "All that counts are two things: If he has basic talent and he wants to listen and learn, I want to teach him."

"I've never known more than two people who could teach hitting and communicate with players, and Doby is one of them,"

Jim Fanning, the first general manager of the Montreal Expos, told the *Montreal Gazette*. "I could hire ten pitching coaches in the next hour, but I could sit here for a month and not find one good batting instructor. Doby has the rare qualities . . . the record, the authority, the patience, the ability to communicate."

Ken Singleton was one of the young Expos players who benefited from Doby's advice. After he belted two homers in a game on August 29, 1972, Singleton credited Doby for his success. "At last, I'm hitting the ball the way Larry has been after me all year to do," Singleton told the *Montreal Gazette*. Doby had instructed the switch-hitting Singleton to "lean into the ball" instead of pulling his body away toward the baselines. Hall of Famer Andre Dawson also praised Doby, who had worked with him in the Instructional League in 1975. "I have to give him a lot of credit for whatever success I have," Dawson said to the *Gazette* in July 1977.

All of the above is solid evidence that a number of general managers in search of a field manager to save their sagging franchises grossly underestimated what Doby could have brought to the table—the multitalented baseball IQ he had expanded even more during his later years as a coach.

But no more managerial offers ever came. He settled into a reluctant retirement, during which he wrote letters to several owners and general managers asking for consideration as various managerial jobs became open.

Meanwhile, his decades-long friendship with Taub, who funded the Doby statue at the rebuilt Larry Doby Field in Paterson; the relationship with Yogi; and the long telephone calls with ex-Eagles teammate Don Newcombe made retirement seemingly acceptable. No longer was the thought of his long-denied election to the Baseball Hall of Fame a vibrant idea to him. He remained, after all, the other guy, the mostly forgotten second man up in the overall battle to integrate baseball, the guy who fell through the cracks while so many writers who should have known better yawned and said, "Old story," without acknowledging how much harder the American League made it for him than the National did for Jackie Robinson.

The most encouragement Doby got in those early days came from a totally unexpected source. Not many among the game's superstars went out of their way to encourage the only Black man in the American League, but Ted Williams did. Williams, the greatest hitter of his era, could be rude to the point of being nasty. He didn't care who or what the object of his ire was.

Back then, the outfielders would leave their gloves on the grass when they came in to hit. In Doby's second year, in a game against the Red Sox, Doby bent down to pick up his glove and got whacked in the ass. When he turned to look, it was Williams, who told him loud and clear, "Keep your head up, rookie—you will make it." That was a rare gesture from a great player, and Doby never forgot it.

Williams read the sports sections every day and when he saw something he believed to be unfair or overly personal, he told off the author, often loudly and profanely, in front of as many people as possible. He could take attitude beyond rudeness. His contempt was clear each time he referred to the Boston sportswriters as the "Knights of the Keyboard." But Williams really understood how lonely and isolated Doby was during his playing days. Long after both men were retired, he bumped into Doby at a chance gathering and said (again loud enough for all nearby to hear), "It's a damn shame you aren't in the Hall of Fame."

Doby smiled. Then Williams added, “Well, we are going to do something about it.”

Doby mumbled a genuine thanks, but in his heart he knew that nobody could.

Well . . . he was wrong.

He didn’t get many votes (partially because of what should have been long-dead prejudice) in the early traditional balloting on which only the working members of the Baseball Writers’ Association of America voted. Beyond prejudice, the key factor had to do with the semireligious mentality of most baseball writers, who treated statistics as though they were Gregorian chants.

My rebuttal in such discussions: “What kind of numbers do you think Babe Ruth or Ty Cobb or any of the big names in the Hall would have put up if they’d had to deal every day with death threats, Jim Crow hotels, water fountains, restaurants, and taxicabs, and anonymous telephone calls to their families?”

Later, as the rules allowed, Doby’s case was moved to the Veterans Committee, where he was casually mentioned for consideration for enshrinement in the Hall. I used my daily column to lobby for his induction. Nothing happened. Doby told me, “It’s not that important. Don’t keep doing it. It won’t happen.”

When he was voted in, I really had nothing to do with it—but I know who did.

I never expected what followed. Before the committee met, I wrote one last column. It was nastier than it should have been. Then I copied it and mailed it to everyone on the committee. My letter began, "I am not surprised that he is not in yet. I am sure that one or two of you didn't want him to play in the first place."

That was stupid. I had no reason and no proof and, I am sure, no impact. I received only one answer:

"Dear asshole:

"Monte Irvin, Yogi Berra and I have been trying to get this done. If you meant to help, then get your ass off the couch and find some votes."

It was signed: Ted Williams.

And Ted, Monte, and Yogi made it happen.

Later that week, I discussed it with Irvin, who had been a good friend of mine for decades and, as Junior told me, often spent time at the Doby home. "It was overdue for so long," Monte said. "He was a great player, the first Black man in the American League, and they gave him a hard road to travel. I wonder how much easier it could have been for him if he had played in, say, New York or Los Angeles or Chicago—media capitals. He reminds me of another great player: Roberto Clemente. As good as both were, because they played in Cleveland and Pittsburgh, they were playing in the shadows."

They had not yet announced the results, and as the target day approached, Larry still could not bring himself to believe it would happen. "I'm going out to California and stay with Newk [Don Newcombe]," he said. "I'm not going to sit home and hope it happens. Let them find me."

So they sat together in Don Newcombe's den and waited and exchanged memories. They were both seventy-two years old, both had played with the Newark Eagles, and both ended their playing careers with the Chunichi Dragons in Nagoya, Japan. Larry never told me what they talked about that day, but between them they had experienced enough triumphs and setbacks to fill a Russian novel.

Newk had conquered alcoholism with such determination that the Dodgers had hired him to counsel players fighting the same battle. The two had a lot to share waiting for Cooperstown to answer this latest riddle.

I reached Doby by phone shortly after the Hall called him.

"I felt relief that this is off my shoulders," he told me. "I never thought it would happen all these years, but then a few people started talking about it and I got to thinking about it. And now it's finally happened. I thank God that I could make it through all those years without losing self-control.

"If I had lost it, who knows if Mr. Veeck might not have been allowed to sign another Black man."

And then, as you might expect, he spoke more about Helyn and the bond between them that helped him endure what no man should have to endure simply because he wanted to play professional baseball. He spoke about his grandmother, Augusta, and his mother, Etta, and the quiet dignity they projected to him, starting in Camden and later Paterson, and the way that dignity carried him through baseball's version of hell.

And then he reminded me of another group, a group neither of us had ever met personally. They changed his life, and he said he would never forget them. In 1947, he suggested there were only two reasons they went to a major-league ballpark for the first time: Jackie Robinson and Larry Doby. "I saw them and I heard them whether I hit a home run, caught a fly ball, or struck out. It was like an ocean of Black faces. This is for them as much as me. They are gonna be in my mind when I step to the microphone in Cooperstown."

As the calendar raced toward July 1998, there were preparations to be made, people to be called. Helyn, he told me, was over the moon with excitement for him. So were the kids. I asked him if he had heard from anyone in Camden. He laughed when he said, "They are the real people. Nineteen of them are coming by chartered bus."

"How will it feel to see Cooperstown again but this time your face is going in on a plaque that will be there forever?"

"I don't know—I've never been there. I never had a reason."

All right, buddy, I thought. *Have I got a surprise for you.*

Cooperstown, New York (population 1,867), is the home of the National Baseball Hall of Fame and Museum, in central New York state, a little more than two hundred miles from New York City. According to the village administration, it was settled in the late eighteenth century. Its aesthetic centerpiece is Otsego Lake and the Otesaga Hotel, which overlooks the lake. The hotel was built in 1909 and is listed in the National Register of Historic Places. It is here Baseball Hall of Fame inductees, including Doby and his family, would live during Hall of Fame Week.

Cooperstown was selected as the site for the Hall because Abner Doubleday, one of several men thought to have actually invented baseball, lived there for a time. I don't know who really invented the game, and I don't think anybody really does, but they couldn't have found a more beautiful setting for its acknowledged shrine. If the village of Cooperstown didn't exist, Norman Rockwell would have painted it as a *Saturday Evening Post* cover and mailed it to the Wizard of Oz to bring it to life. They just don't make villages in America like that anymore.

On induction day each year, the town is packed. Across from the baseball museum, a US Postal Service trailer sells canceled Hall of Fame postage stamps as keepsakes. Eateries and baseball souvenir shops line Main Street, leading up to the Hall itself. The ceremonies used to be held on the lawn in front of the red-bricked Hall of Fame, but the crowds got so large that it was moved to a spacious municipal park called the Clark Sports Center.

His wife's side of the family would do the driving from New Jersey. But down in Camden, South Carolina, nineteen Dobys were signing up for a chartered bus trip to the Cooperstown ceremony. They would assemble at the Camden Archives and Museum, near the statue of native son Larry Doby. The travelers would arrive the morning of the ceremony and leave right after it was over. That's more than twenty-five hours on a bus.

Halfway around the world, in Perth, Australia, Larry Doby Jr. was at work constructing the set for a Billy Joel concert. He had been a member of the entertainer's road crew for a long time. He was amazed when somebody hollered at him, "Hey, the boss wants you in his office right now."

"I was stunned," Junior told me. "I mean, what did I do wrong that he needed to see me? I felt like I was back in high school and I had been told I needed to go to the principal's office. I walked in and he told me to sit down. He had been reading an issue of *USA Today*. He handed me his newspaper.

"'Did you see this yet?'" he asked. It was the announcement that his dad had been voted into the Hall.

"At first, I was more shocked than anything. Just a year earlier, there had been talk he might get in. Then nothing happened. We knew he was disappointed. He was positive he would never be chosen. So we [the family] stopped talking about it in respect to him. But after the shock, I felt like a wave of joy had washed over me."

The day I arrived in Cooperstown, I stopped by the Hall to see Jeff Idelson. He was then the organization's vice president of communications and education, a role that included overseeing the Hall of Fame's day-to-day operations. I asked him for a favor. He granted it. He would close the museum on time at 9 p.m. one night and then reopen it an hour later for Doby and me.

Larry and Helyn drove to Cooperstown with their daughters. Junior arrived separately. Two days before the ceremony, Larry and I had lunch at the Otesaga.

"I hope you and Helyn don't have any plans for tonight," I said. "I have a little surprise for you. After the museum closes tonight, you and I are going to take our own tour. Just us alone. We can take as long as you want. The ladies can sit in the lobby. Meet us there after nine tonight."

They were waiting for us when we arrived. Larry wore a multicolored knit polo shirt and dark slacks.

The ladies, who knew one another, sat in the lobby and talked. A custodian told us how to contact him when we had finished so he could lock up.

A few steps inside, and then we were all alone in the belly of the beast. Alone with all that had happened before Doby signed to play for Veeck . . . alone in a world of history that formed a mountain of the way it was and the way it now struggled to be.

We stood at the edge of history soon to be revealed. Each display case filled with images of the game seemed to bear witness to a time when nobody Black mailed threats to a city about moving out unless they got a new municipal-financed stadium, a time when every town and hamlet sandlot team had its own July 4 doubleheader.

Long after the Baseball Hall of Fame's closing time, its newest initiate wandered its halls, thinking private thoughts, measuring the pieces of his professional life in a way that only those who are among the chosen can do.

In the surrounding silence, the echo of our footsteps through the empty halls seemed to offer a ghostly welcome to the new man. In forty-eight hours, his plaque goes up. In forty-eight hours, the journey is finished.

We had walked in silence until we reached the main rotunda and a series of alcoves with honoree plaques mounted on the walls. Among them he discovered the one bearing the image of Bill Veeck, the man who paid $15,000 to Effa Manley for his Newark Eagles contract. The man who took both of their names into history.

He stared at the plaque as though he were checking every detail, and then he laughed. "They got it," he said. "That look. It was like he was always in a hurry for the next challenge."

We passed a Negro Leagues section. He felt they did not give his Eagles enough credit. Occasionally, he turned to me and commented on an old glove, a faded Homestead Grays poster. Each in its own way evoked a memory or a comment, and as we passed memorabilia of the greatest of the great, he couldn't help but reflect on some who were just as good but who were born too soon for a seat at the table.

"Great Black men, like my Eagles teammates Ray Dandridge and Leon Day, never had the shot I got. There was just no quit in those guys. They could be 10 runs down and expect to win."

When he mentioned Leon's name, I recalled a story Monte Irvin had told me. He had been Day's roommate with the Eagles, but one winter in the Puerto Rican League they played against each other. After the games they would head home and rejoin the Eagles. Monte told me Leon was a guy full of jokes and laughter, but when he looked down from the mound at a hitter, his face would change.

"The first pitch, he throws me high and tight—and I'm in the dirt on my face," Irvin recalled. "So I yell at him, 'Are you crazy? Tomorrow we'll be back as roommates for the Eagles? And I ain't hittin' but .256 down here.' He looks back at me like he don't even know me and he yells, 'That's tomorrow, but you ain't leaving this island hittin' .257!'"

Doby laughed. "That's the way we all were. We weren't trying to prove anything to major-league scouts because there weren't any looking at us. . . . We played the game for each other."

By then we were back in the center of the building. It was as though the sound of those ghostly footsteps was guiding us to a place we had to see. Suddenly, we were there.

We stood in front of an exhibit that featured a team picture of his 1948 world champion Cleveland Indians.

He pointed. "There he is." Doby shook his head slowly and grunted—he was pointing at the manager, Lou Boudreau. For a moment I thought he was going say "The son of a bitch." But I never heard him curse—never, although he was entitled to do so, over and over.

He just grunted again, and the second grunt spoke volumes. Then his finger was moving again. When it stopped, he unleashed a rainbow of a grin—he was pointing at Joe Gordon, his warm-up partner and closest mate. "The best teammate I ever had—anywhere."

We were moving slowly through the artifacts of a dream once denied him, a dream then deferred and, tomorrow, in this same little village, a dream whose time had finally come. Tomorrow would be television cameras and a huge press conference and all the right words spoken before an adoring audience just up the road, sunshine and good memories and the Doby family awash in pride for their dad, Helyn Doby's husband.

We were coming to the evening's end. The magical mystery tour was over as we stood near the exit and the women left the lobby bench and came toward us.

"So what do you think now?" I asked as he leaned forward to open the exit door.

"I will never forget this night," Doby said.

As we turned to leave, he went on. "When it looked as though I'd never get here, I used to tell myself it didn't matter. But tonight I realize how much it means to me. It is time to put all the negatives behind. We all know what they were. It is time to think about the positives now. There are people nobody acknowledges. Happy Chandler, for example, was the commissioner. Everybody says 'Southerner' and stereotypes him. But he had the guts to approve Mr. Robinson's contract, and weeks later he approved mine."

It was a surprisingly insightful comment, the only time he ever mentioned Chandler to me. Maybe it was the magic of the night. A night without pressure . . . a night to realize how far he had come . . . a rare night that truly belonged to him. On this night he walked alone among myths and legends.

Within forty-eight hours, he would become one of them.

CHAPTER 14

SIX MINUTES TO GLORY

My wife, Aileen, and I had an early breakfast in a Main Street eatery. Across the street, they were already lining up at the US Postal trailer to purchase souvenir postage stamps memorializing the 1998 induction ceremonies. The baseball memorabilia shops were packed. On Main Street the sidewalks were crowded with slow-moving family traffic.

A week earlier you could have shot off a cannon and not hit anyone. This was a dose of the village's annual magic. Where did all these people come from? It reminded me of a scene from the Broadway musical hit *Brigadoon*, about the sleepy mythical Scottish village that hibernates in the mist and comes to life for one day every hundred years.

Exaggeration?

Maybe not.

This is the day Larry Doby becomes an overnight sensation at age seventy-four. The chartered bus moving up Main Street was filled with nineteen Dobys: young, old, and in between, three generations' worth, straight from Camden, South Carolina.

After our late-night tour of the Hall of Fame, I asked Doby about his coming speech—was he going to mention the Black doctor who befriended him and was murdered at a lunch counter sit-in?

Larry had given that a lot of thought. "I'm not sure yet. This might not be the time and place for it. No more negatives. It's time for positives. There are people and there are memories, and I know I will think about all of them just before that moment takes over."

The doctor? "Well, the Indians and the Giants barnstormed through the South in spring training each year. My second season we stopped at Columbus, Georgia, where, of course, I couldn't stay in the all white hotel. After the game, a Black doctor named Alexander took me in. I wish I could recall his first name. His family made a home for me with them. That was in 1948, '49, and '50. He was a beautiful man.

"Ten years later . . . he went down to the local lunch counter at J. J. Newberry and sat in to get service for Blacks. He was murdered on his stool.

"Part of today will be for him.

"But there will be no more negatives. It's time to honor the positives: Bill Veeck, who signed me in the face of the owners' rage . . . Happy Chandler, the commissioner, whom nobody talks about but who had the courage to approve my contract . . . teammates like Joe Gordon, who never saw color. It's time we spoke of them."

And he did, in the greatest six-minute speech I ever heard.

Six minutes. That's all his moment in the sun would take. But the huge crowd was spellbound.

Six minutes for Larry Doby to put a magnificent punctuation mark on an incredible journey that began in a league where only the ball was white but the camaraderie was real . . . that took an agonizingly lonely turn through the guts of a baseball purgatory that only one other man, Jackie Robinson, will have ever shared . . . and that concluded in a burst of redemption on a portable stage in an emerald-green meadow barely a mile from the village where Major League Baseball built its pantheon.

As I sat in that beautiful park waiting for his speech, I wondered, as I had for years, how this remarkable man who was dealt such a lousy hand by a little boys' game played for money by grown men, a deal that perverted the lifestyle it offered him, how he never hated the people and business that fostered it.

I couldn't have handled it. And I never knew anyone but Jackie and Larry who could. Then Bud Selig, the commissioner, was at the microphone introducing Larry Doby.

Doby gave us six minutes that were fifty-one years in the making. Six minutes, twice interrupted by lengthy, emotional applause that echoed across the soft undulation of sun-drenched green expanse, hurled itself at the stage in a joyous chorus, and served as the ruffles and flourishes with which Larry Doby marched into the Baseball Hall of Fame.

It was a 360-second tableau for the ages—for baseball, for history, for justice. Fathers who hadn't even been born when Doby crossed the American League's color line in 1947 held their children high in the air as if to say, "Remember this man. Remember his words. Remember this day."

Doby was determined that this would be a day of positives, and his speech reflected that notion. But long before the day arrived, he confided to me that there were things that needed to be said.

So this was the way it was when he set out for the ceremony, a ceremony that would end with a bronze plaque and his own corner in the Hall of Fame. But, more important, it would end with a kind of redemption for baseball itself, for recognizing the truth at last.

They had assembled on the stage one by one—inductees from baseball's past, from Yogi to Stan the Man, from Sandy Koufax to Phil Niekro. And then suddenly, with no announcement and no fanfare, the Class of '98 slipped into the front row, stage left.

There was ninety-four-year-old Sam Lacy, the Black journalist to whom Doby's enshrinement was every bit as important as his own. (Gordon Cobbledick wrote in a Cleveland newspaper that Doby's thoughts that a pitcher threw at him because of race were Doby's version of playing the race card. So Lacy went out, proved the writer wrong, and printed it for the world to read.)

The others were Jaime Jarrín, the man who gave Los Angeles Dodgers radio its Spanish voice; the Kansas City Monarchs' "Bullet" Joe Rogan (represented onstage by his son Wilber), who was born too soon to crack the color line and who died too soon to know he was appreciated; Lee MacPhail Jr., an honored baseball executive from a renowned baseball family; Don Sutton, a well-traveled right-handed pitcher whose time had finally come.

And, of course, Larry Doby.

He wore a navy-blue suit, a gold and red tie, and sunglasses. The former wartime sailor stood at a thoughtful "parade rest" as the words cut through the brilliant afternoon sun. Donna Greenwald, a woman with a beautiful voice, sang:

Oh, say, can you see by the dawn's early light . . .

How many times had he heard the same words in the little ballpark in Newark while Leon Day or Max Manning finished warming up in the left field bullpen and the Eagles stood shoulder-to-shoulder in freshly laundered white uniforms, holding a royal-blue cap with the script "E" over his heart?

. . . what so proudly we hailed . . .

How easy it must have been for him to conjure up the image of that weary concrete saucer called Cleveland Municipal Stadium on a humid summer night with the wind blowing in off Lake Erie while Bob Feller was warming up and Doby was about to go out and play center field.

. . . o'er the land of the free and the home of the brave.

And you had to wonder how many years and in how many parks in the heat of the sun or the glare of the arc lights had he heard those words? And how many times in the segregated hotels and locker rooms denied to him did he wonder when they would apply to him?

But of course all of that was long dead when he mounted the podium. This was a man who never hated. Hate is a dead thing at best, and Larry Doby refused to live in a tomb.

Long ago, he had told me, "I hear all this talk about how bad baseball is on race relations, but, you know, all I have to say about that is, go look at the country and go look at baseball and tell me which one has come the furthest. I wound up in baseball because Mr. Veeck signed me—not because of legislation."

There are only four men who ever played in both the Negro Leagues World Series and the MLB World Series: Monte Irvin, Willie Mays, Satchel Paige, and Larry Doby. On this day, the speech he delivered was for all of them.

Standing tall at the podium, in those six minutes, he accentuated the positive as perhaps no graduate of the Negro Leagues before him had, and as nobody who had not experienced it could have.

When he moved out of the row of new inductees to receive his plaque from Bud Selig, there was a marvelous dignity to his bearing. This was a moment that had looked as though it would never come. But now it was here, and now this crowd that cared nothing about the politics of baseball and did not know nearly enough about its history did know one thing, and it acted accordingly after he opened with a simple declaration of who he was.

He began:

"I come from a little town in South Carolina named Camden."

The crowd rose to its feet in tribute. It knew it was in the presence of class, and that the statistics the commissioner reeled off had been achieved under the most onerous of burdens, and that the only other man who could measure that was the only other man who had actually lived it: Jackie Robinson.

But Larry Doby was teaching them what America needed to know about himself and the untold story that for decades had been his alone. It knew this man, this outfielder, was a special baseball man stepping forward on the most special of baseball days. In six minutes, he proved that all over again.

It triggered with a twenty-nine-second spontaneous standing ovation. He acknowledged his family and then he spoke of the others: of "Mr. Veeck and Mr. Robinson" and Commissioner Happy Chandler. Then he acknowledged the presence of Veeck's widow in the audience. He crammed all the people he could into one thought about Camden, South Carolina, where he was born, and Paterson, New Jersey, where he was raised, and the Eagles, with whom he learned, and the Indians, with whom he graduated.

Then he said, "You know, it's a very tough thing to look back about things that were probably negative. [On such a day] you put those things on the back burner. You are proud and happy that you've been a part of integrating baseball to show people that we can live together, we can work together, and we can be successful together."

At that point, the huge crowd delivered sixteen more seconds of emotional, foot-stamping ovation. And months later, he still spoke of Helyn's reaction. "I have never seen her so happy. She was jumping around and cheering and clapping her hands like a little kid. I couldn't take my eyes off her. I have never seen her so happy. I watched her every move."

It was as though on that day she and Doby clearly shared a basic truth that Black and white America had yet to learn.

I still think a lot about that day in Cooperstown and the positive emotions that were alive in that crowd. Obviously you could hear it in the thunder of their appreciative responses. You could see it in their expressions and their smiles. In that instant there was a kind of positive unity that seemed to say, "Thank you—now we finally understand."

That, in itself, may be the mark of what sports could mean to America—if sports only understood the real power for understanding that they could unleash.

For proof, I refer you to Arthur Ashe, who did understand, and who wrote in his book *A Hard Road to Glory: A History of the African-American Athlete* that, "These and others [athletes] have been the most accomplished figures in the African-American subculture. They were vastly better known in their times than people such as Booker T. Washington, William E.B. Du Bois, or

Marcus Garvey. They inspired idolatry bordering on deification, and thousands more wanted to follow."

So how could a player this good and a man this genuine be permitted to fall far between the cracks of history for so long? The best answer may be found in a quote that biographer Joe Moore attributed to Buck O'Neil, the great Kansas City Monarchs first baseman, who played against Doby in the 1946 Negro League World Series:

"I believe I would have made Larry one of the greatest players who ever lived. There were a whole lot of rough spots he had to face. He's a beautiful person, but few people know him."

If they don't know him now, they should have been in Cooperstown that afternoon.

CHAPTER 15
THE MEASURE OF A MAN

He never changed. Not when Ted Williams called to tell him that the Veterans Committee had announced his long-overdue election to the Hall of Fame, not when he stepped to the podium and could have said whatever he wanted about the inexplicable years when baseball chose to forget what he did . . . and not when the commissioner handed him the plaque.

He never measured his life in symbols. He walked in dignity and in fairness—even when the game he loved ignored the love he gave it. Had Bill Veeck not brought him to the majors, had he played his entire career as a Newark Eagle, marking the days in long bus rides, low salaries, and cheap hotels, he would have been the same Larry Doby—a secret hero, revered only in the eyes of the Black community.

Right?

Well, he was just a baseball player. And Miles Davis just played the trumpet, and Arthur Ashe just played tennis, and Billie Holiday just sang songs.

But all of them proved that you don't need a paint brush to be an artist. Davis played "My Funny Valentine" as it has never been played before. Arthur Ashe won the US Open and shocked the tennis world. Billie Holiday sang "Strange Fruit" and changed the civil rights movement.

And Larry Doby spit in the face of Jim Crow as the first Black man to homer in a World Series and gave the American League a dignity it never deserved. All he did was make a fool out of George Weiss, the man who ran the Yankees, who'd achieved infamy with his response about whether he would sign a Black player ("Our fans are different. Do you think a Wall Street stockbroker would buy season box-seat tickets to see a colored boy play for us?").

Right? Who needed Larry Doby or Willie Mays or Hank Aaron or Don Newcombe?

I still look at the preprinted credo Doby used on his autographed pictures in a line of yellow type: "I cannot change yesterday. I can only make the most of today, and look with hope toward tomorrow."

He not only never forgot that thought, he lived it.

After the induction ceremony, he went back to Montclair and the things he most prized, his wife and kids. One of them, Larry Jr., would play professional baseball. His relationship with the Veeck family remained strong. He took part in fifteen ceremonies at Mike Veeck's ballparks honoring Veeck's dad and Doby. He played golf and lived his life, but most of all he remained a symbol of hope in his New Jersey blue-collar world.

I had founded an organization called Project Pride to help disadvantaged children in Newark. Like Doby, those kids were the forgotten ones, the ones for whom nobody seemed to care.

Larry Sr. was on my board of directors. He was active in our SAT class. He helped merchandise our football game fundraiser that sent 1,100 Newark kids to college.

One day during game week, he handed me a white envelope.

"What's in this thing?"

"Try opening it."

There was a check made out to Project Pride for $1,000, with his signature.

"Listen, you have done so much," I said. "It's enough. I can't take this check."

He glared at me in mock anger. Then he burst out laughing. "So that's how it is? The white man is still telling the Black man how he can spend his money. Take it."

I did.

In 1997, decades after Doby's final at-bat, New Jersey Representative William Pascrell suggested naming the main post office in Paterson after Doby. The Postal Service also struck a stamp with his image. That same year, Princeton and Fairfield universities bestowed honorary doctorates on him. In earlier and later years, South Carolina, New Jersey, and the Cleveland Indians inducted him into their respective Halls of Fame. And although he passed away twenty years before it happened, he was awarded the Congressional Gold Medal in 2023.

On the medal's reverse side is the famous photo of Doby and teammate Steve Gromek hugging after Doby's home run in the 1948 World Series, the first such interracial photo to appear on the front pages of America's newspapers. The Dobys and the Gromeks insisted on its depiction on the medal.

Those were among the times of the life and love affair of Larry and Helyn Doby. Now, without distraction, they had time for each other. Time to totally share.

And then as quickly as the good times arrived, they were gone.

Helyn Curvy Doby passed away on July 19, 2001, at age seventy-six.

Larry died on June 18, 2003, at age seventy-nine.

"Black, White, or Asian," Doby's last surviving high school football teammate, Al Kachadurian, once told me, "Helyn Curvy was the prettiest girl in school. Larry Doby was her boyfriend. He was good looking and the best athlete Eastside High School ever had. To us, they were what the kids today call a power couple. Everyone wanted to be them."

Larry Doby was voted into the Hall in 1998, and Helyn passed three years later, just when they had some breathing room in their post-baseball life, a brand-new time when they could finally erase all the distractions and concentrate on each other.

It was a love affair that lasted more than half a century. After she passed, Larry and I were sitting in his den and he was trying to express the depth of his loss. How do you explain the intensity of losing the only partner you had ever loved?

He stared for a long, frozen moment at the wall where his uniform jersey with the big No. 14 was on display. Then he looked back at me. The master bedroom was directly behind the den.

"I sleep here," he said, patting the couch. "After all those years, more than fifty, I just can't sleep in there in that room alone."

Two years later, after Doby passed away, Mike Veeck, whose father was the architect of the great experiment that catapulted Doby across the American League color line, said, with great feeling, "I don't know if there is an afterlife. I hope so, because it surely would mean Larry and Helyn are together again."

I never understood the strange roadblock that separated Jackie Robinson from Larry Doby in the illogical collective mind of baseball's self-styled heavyweight thinkers. Jim Crow is always Jim Crow. It doesn't live by accident. It doesn't matter who had it harder.

What only mattered was that both of them fought hatred alone against odds nobody beat in those days. The legacy, anger, and resistance the National League threw at Jackie were based on the league's slavish devotion to an irrational tradition that America's game had shared for a century.

But based on the history of the American League and the openly stated rhetoric of the men who owned it, it occurs to me that the anger directed at Doby was 24-karat racism in its most evil, arrogant form. It was not an accident that the Boston Red Sox were the last team in all of baseball to sign a Black player.

The words of George Weiss, Calvin Griffith, Tom Yawkey, as quoted in this book, are strong self-indictments.

When baseball retired Jackie Robinson's No. 42 forever in both leagues, it was an honor gladly bestowed. When Cleveland retired Doby's No. 14, no other team followed suit.

Why? Both of them broke color lines. Doby was alone in his own league even more than Jackie was in his. Most of the media in the American League either ignored him or, as was the case with two influential writers in Cleveland, blamed him for his team's failures, or charged him with using his race as a crutch for self-pity.

But all the voices behind the negativity are gone today. Ironically, he served as an executive aide to Gene Budig, the last American League president before that job was abolished. Baseball needs to do something to tell the world that what Doby achieved changed the complexion of the American League and America.

Someone, I don't recall who it was, once proposed a Doby shoulder patch to be worn by every American League team once a year, on the anniversary of his signing. But the league has never even discussed any kind of lasting honor for the man who by himself forced it to integrate.

For too long, he has been baseball's invisible hero.

OBITUARY OF LARRY DOBY, BY JERRY IZENBERG

Strength and Dignity Delivered Doby to Greatness
The *Star-Ledger* (Newark, New Jersey), June 19, 2003
By Jerry Izenberg

LARRY DOBY, 1924–2003
Death be not proud, though some have called thee mighty, and dreadful, for thou art not so, for those whom thou thinkest thou dost overthrow, die not. . . . —John Donne, "Death Be Not Proud"

This is the way Larry Doby left us. The doctors long ago knew the medical count on him was 0-2. He lost a kidney . . . but he went out and played golf. He fought the pain of cancer . . . but he kept visiting schools in Newark and Paterson to remind the kids for whom he cared so much that it's not how you start but how you finish.

He took the treatments, he fought a slow, painful battle against fatigue . . . but even then he laughed on the telephone and he shared memories and he never, ever, ever complained.

And all the while there was that obscenity called Death, which has no shame and no pride, standing on the mound, jeering, loading up another spitball, and hollering, "You can't win. Why don't you quit?"

And in the back roads of Larry's mind he kept picking up the pitcher's release with eyes that were born to see fastballs, fouling off pitch after pitch, with that incredibly fluid swing, grinding his spikes deeper into the dirt, staring out at a pitcher nobody else could see and daring him with his last breath:

"Go ahead, meat. Bring it. Bring the heat. Bring the junk. It's all the same to me. You want me? You gotta do better than that."

He died yesterday . . . but not his legacy . . . not his gift to all of us.

He was as gentle as he was tough. He was as realistic as he was sensitive. And, above all, he was tested, perhaps more than anyone I ever knew.

Looking back, he was a hero to everyone except himself.

Historians never really got it. He was the second African-American to play in the majors, the first in the American League. But after Jackie, revisionists would have you believe it was all over. This was, after all, America, they reasoned in their footnotes. This was, after all, baseball.

Doby came to Cleveland six weeks after Jackie had come to Brooklyn. But unlike Jackie, he remained alone for a long, long time. The American League, in contravention to its very name, integrated with the speed of a herniated inchworm.

Bill Veeck, who may have been the most decent human being ever to own a ball club, signed him out of the Negro National League, where he played for the Newark Eagles. Their friendship continued right up until Veeck's death years later. They shared a lot: baseball, the game they both loved; late-night jazz, the music to which they listened together on nights when Veeck made surprise visits to whatever city the Indians were in because he wanted to ease the lonely pain that was Doby's only companion that year.

Decades after it was over, we would sit and talk, and little by little he tried to explain the way it was—sometimes unleashing long-gone pain that he had held inside for far too long. One night, he sat in my living room and explained to me the real meaning of humiliation. He told me about the moment the manager, Lou Boudreau, who didn't want him, introduced him to the players who wanted him even less. He had just joined the club:

"I walked down that line, stuck out my hand, and very few hands came back in return. Most of the ones that did were cold-fish handshakes, along with a look that said, 'You don't belong here.'

"I grew up in a mixed neighborhood in Paterson. I ate in my classmates' homes and they ate in mine. I was the only Black on the football team, and when we were invited to play segregated high school bowl games in Florida, the team voted to stay home rather than play without me.

"Now, I couldn't believe how this was. I put on my uniform and I went out on the field to warm up, but nobody wanted to warm up with me. I had never been so alone in my life. I stood there alone in front of the dugout for five minutes. Then Joe Gordon, the second baseman who would become my friend, came up to me and asked, 'Hey, rookie, you gonna just stand there or do you want to throw a little?'

"I will never forget that man."

The next day, Boudreau told him he wanted him to start at first base. He had no first baseman's glove. Eddie Robinson, the regular first baseman, refused to lend him his. The team's traveling secretary had to walk over to the other team's dugout to borrow one.

He lived in the kind of dugout Jackie never knew.

Another night, he talked about the isolation . . . about being barred from the front entrance to stadiums in St. Louis and Washington. He spoke of the malevolent beanballs thrown behind him, the infielder who spit tobacco juice in his face, the spring training bus trips when he sat in the bus after games while his teammates ate in restaurants and when Gordon would say—as he always did—"'I'm so sorry about this. Can I bring you a sandwich or something, L.D.?'" Doby recalled.

"I'd be sitting on the bus hungry as a son of a bitch," Doby said. "But I'd tell him to forget it. I wasn't going to spend one damn penny with those sons of bitches."

On another night he told me, "I always hit well in Washington and St. Louis. I saw them out in the Jim Crow seats. I felt like a high school quarterback with his own 5,000 cheerleaders. I knew who was making the noise and exactly where it was coming from. And I will tell you they made some noise. When I hit a home run, their sound was deafening."

He remembered the beer bottles thrown at the back of his head during an exhibition game down South, the boos and the curses and how he hit the longest home run in the history of the park that day and the roar from the Jim Crow seats that was a message to keep on keepin' on.

He was my friend, and the longer I knew him and watched the way he easily moved in any kind of social circle, I would ask myself—but never him—*How could he keep from hating?* I know that had it been me, I could not.

I began to figure it out the night before he was inducted into the Baseball Hall of Fame, in 1998. I arranged for the two us to walk through the empty building alone after closing.

He paused repeatedly and conducted his own nonstop soliloquy about the exhibits and the game he loved. His heart smiled at some of those memories. His silence spoke volumes at some of the other ones. I finally understood that night just how much he loved this game and why, with all the heartache, it remained forever a part of his life.

He had paused before a picture of Steve Gromek, a pitcher on Doby's 1948 world championship Indians, leaping into Doby's arms. Larry had hit a home run in that World Series game and Gromek had been the winning pitcher.

"It made most of the front pages," he told me. "It was the first picture of a Black and aWhite man embracing at home plate. America needed that picture, and I will always be proud that I could help give it to them."

He filled in the blanks the next day with an induction speech that made me cry when I thought of all he had been through and the dignity and laughter with which he had handled his life. In that, I was not alone. He looked the world in the eye that sun-drenched afternoon and offered it a basic truth when at the finish he said, "You know, it is very tough to look back on things that were negative. [On such a day] you put those things on the back burner and you are proud and happy that you were a part of integrating baseball to show people that we can live together, we can work together and we can be successful together."

He was delivering a truth that the rest of much of America, Black and White, has yet to learn.

All his life, he brought a new dimension to grace under pressure. He never forgot who he was. He knew what was important: courage, dignity, caring, and family.

I already miss him.

EPILOGUE

"Kids are our future, and we hope baseball has given them some idea of what it is to live together and how we can get along, whether you be Black or white."

—Larry Doby

We had a group called Project Pride, and each year we ran a college football game to fund the seventeen programs we sponsored for Newark kids. Larry Doby was on our board of directors, and we sent 1,100 local kids to college. On April 23, 1997, we honored him as our Man of the Year.

When he was introduced, he couldn't speak for about a minute because the standing ovation he received lasted about twenty-five seconds. This was in West Orange, New Jersey, about five miles from his home in Montclair. The ovation proved that for all the time baseball may have forgotten him, New Jersey didn't.

Because he waited so long in Jackie Robinson's shadow, people who did not know him thought he was bitter. They were wrong. The first thing he said that night proved who he really was. When the applause stopped, he said, "Where were you guys when I needed you?" And then he laughed, and it was clear that bitterness was somebody else's burden.

When he passed away on June 18, 2003, at the age of seventy-nine, baseball seemed to rediscover him. The Associated Press wire was jammed with tributes. Some were heartfelt, some were emotional, and some were obligatory and, therefore, hollow. A judgment of what they said and why and how they said it, I leave to the reader.

But when you dig through all the superlatives, the real tribute shines through in the rhetoric of a lady from Camden, South Carolina, where Doby was born. She didn't care for baseball at all and never saw him play. Her tribute was something he would have liked to hear. People like her were the ones he wanted to reach.

Ms. Elizabeth Robinson (no relation to Jackie), a retired kindergarten teacher, was a volunteer at the town's Afro-American Cultural Center, which some time ago unveiled a Larry Doby exhibit. She didn't know much about Doby and didn't care to learn anything at all about baseball.

But one day when she forgot to bring her phone and her knitting needles to the center, she decided to tour the Doby exhibit on her own. It made a major impact on her.

"I'm interested in baseball now," she said, "and I have so much more respect for Larry Doby.

"The other night I was flipping through the TV channels and baseball came on. I did something I have never done before in my entire life. I thought about Mr. Doby, and I watched the game."

EPILOGUE

Bill Veeck died on January 2, 1986, at the age of seventy-one. Baseball has never had an owner to match his imagination, his humanity, and his respect for the fans in the cheap seats. Veeck and Larry Doby, even in death, remain linked forever even now. The day after Larry died, Libby Veeck, Bill's daughter-in-law and Mike's wife, sent this letter to the Doby children:

Dearest Doby children -

Jerry called tonight to deliver the sad news of your dads death.. We knew it was coming, we knew he was ready. We know that he has rejoined the love of his life. I'm sure his only sadness was that he had to leave his children. I know how much he loves all of you - and how proud he was. Rightfully so. It's the mark of loving parents to build a family like you were lucky enough to have.

Your dad was one of the most remarkable people I've been lucky enough to meet in my lifetime. Knowing what he had to endure only made him more heroic in my eyes. Knowing it is one thing, but actually living it is something I simply cannot imagine. Your mom was able to give me a better understanding of the pain and humiliation they were forced to live with. I hope you find comfort in knowing that your dad made it a better world to live in. He was a prince among men.

One of my fondest memories will be spending his last Cooperstown reunion with your family. He was in his glory and so proud to have his girls there with him. It was then that he told me how sick able to come and visit our home. I'll never forget his kindness to our daughter Rebecca and how well they got along. She like all of us adored him. Heavens gain is our loss.

Michael + I will not be returning to Cooperstown this year. It will never be the same without him.

I could go on forever, but I'm sure you know how we feel. Please let's stay in touch.

All our love –

The Michael Veech family

ACKNOWLEDGMENTS

A number of people made contributions without which this book never would have happened. First and foremost was the exchange of ideas that persisted between Larry Doby and me over four decades; the help from his son, Larry Doby Jr., and his love for his father; Mike Veeck, whose mother and dad, and he himself, were the glue that held the Doby family and the Veeck family together; Al Kachadurian, who threw the passes Doby caught on his state-champion Paterson Eastside High School football team and knew him better than any other high school teammate; Len Zax, who recreated for me the Paterson of Larry Doby's youth; the family of the late Steve Gromek; US Congressman Bill Pascrell, who remembered Doby's struggle when others chose to forget; Benjamin Rich, Pascrell's chief of staff; the late Monte Irvin, the late Bill White, and the late Yogi Berra; Jim Overmyer; most of all, my muse, wife, and best friend, Aileen Izenberg; Fred Sternburg, my town crier, who draws attention to the idea that I don't have to write about balls and strikes to be heard; Tom Walsh, the master of both syntax and research, whose editing once again protected me from the grammar police; Peter Sawyer, my agent, and last but never least, Bob Izenberg, my son, who always atones for my computer glitches.